YOU CAN'T GO WRONG DOING RIGHT

YOU CAN'T GO WRONG DOING RIGHT

How a Child of Poverty

Rose to the White House and

Helped Change the World

ROBERT J. BROWN

Convergent
New York

Library of Congress Cataloging-in-Publication Data is available upon request.

ISBN 978-1-5247-6278-0
Ebook ISBN 978-1-5247-6279-7

Printed in the United States of America

Jacket design by Jessie Sayward Bright
Jacket photographs: (first row, left and right; third row, left; fourth row, left and
right) Courtesy of the author; (second row, left) Historical/Getty Images; (second
row, right) Bob Parent/Getty Images; (third row, right) Richard Nixon Presidential
Library and Museum, National Archives and Records Administration

10 9 8 7 6 5 4 3 2 1

First Edition

This book is dedicated to Miss Nellie Brown, my grandmother who raised me and was always "Mama" to me and my brother. Your unconditional love shaped my life and gave me the courage to believe in myself. In addition, your words of wisdom taught me to trust in God and never lose faith in His purpose for my life. Those words continue to guide me even today.

And to my beloved Sallie, my best friend and wife for 47 years. From our childhoods, you were my soul mate, and the love of my life. All that I've accomplished and experienced would have been impossible without your wisdom and support. You will forever be in my heart and soul.

*Everybody can be great . . . because anybody can
serve. You don't have to have a college degree to serve.
You don't have to make your subject and verb agree
to serve. You only need a heart full of grace. A soul
generated by love.*

—The Reverend Martin Luther King Jr.

*You should be angry. You must not be bitter.
Bitterness is like cancer. It eats upon the host.
It doesn't do anything to the object of its displeasure.
So, use that anger. You write it. You paint it.
You dance it. You march it. You vote it. You do
everything about it. You talk it. Never stop talking it.*

—Maya Angelou

Contents

Foreword

I WAS IN MY EARLY THIRTIES AND STILL SEARCHING FOR MY identity when I first met Bob Brown. I'd grown up in a small town, in a working-class family, but I'd played basketball in college and in Europe, and I'd served overseas in the military. So I'd seen some of the world and known all sorts of people, but I'd never met a man like him.

Over the years, I've heard many people say similar things—that they've never met anyone like Robert J. Brown. He is a humble person, yet he is also among the most accomplished and statesmanlike individuals you will ever know.

Oprah and I were introduced to Bob and his wife, Sallie, in the mid-1980s by Dr. Maya Angelou. I was drawn to Bob by his calm demeanor and the confident way he carried himself.

Sallie, who is now deceased, had been Bob's anchor since the second grade. They were a tremendous team.

Though soft-spoken and low-key, Bob radiates intelligence and kindness. I soon learned that he has an extraordinary gift for building lasting relationships across all economic, social, racial, and political lines. He navigates with ease in the halls of power, at backyard barbecues, and through the most challenging crises.

Bob has been a father figure, a mentor, a role model, and a friend to me. He taught me with his words and in his actions that we are defined not by our circumstances but by our possibilities. He helped me develop a greater vision for my life. His influence has made it possible for me to write eleven books, to start and run my own business, and to teach, lecture, and conduct identity leadership workshops around the world.

Bob Brown has been a positive example to many of us. He grew up in poverty, but thanks to the love and support of his grandmother Miss Nellie Brown, Bob rose to become a successful businessman with Fortune 500 clients. During his White House years, he was, arguably, one of the most influential men in the country, African American or otherwise.

Bob has always been a bridge builder as well as a change agent. During his tenure in Washington, DC, he helped lead fundamental and lasting policy changes that have elevated the lives of African Americans and other people. He directed millions of previously withheld federal dollars to historically black colleges and universities. He also fought to promote the first generations of black generals and admirals in every branch of the U.S. military.

Backed by the president and other allies, Bob pushed to create greater educational, career, and financial opportunities for those who'd long been marginalized and denied access to the American Dream.

Prior to his White House service, Bob was a valuable asset to the Reverend Martin Luther King Jr. and other leaders of the civil rights movement. After his White House years, he was equally important as a confidant, benefactor, and—as you will read—fierce advocate for the Mandela family.

Bob Brown's efforts to help the Mandela family and the people of South Africa are, themselves, incredible achievements. Many poor children there and throughout Africa have learned to read and expand their knowledge thanks to his BookSmart Foundation and his desire to get books into the hands of those who had no other access to them.

Though he has always operated out of his hometown headquarters in High Point, North Carolina, Bob has had corporate clients including Sara Lee, USAA, General Motors, Coca-Cola, Nissan, Michelin, Lowe's, AutoNation, Freddie Mac, Sprint, and De Beers.

In addition, Bob Brown, the great-grandson of a slave, has served on the corporate boards of AutoNation, Wachovia Bank, Duke Energy, Blue Ridge Holdings, and Sonoco Products.

I have often heard people say to him, "Mr. Brown, you are one of the most accomplished men no one has ever heard of. Your story should be told." This inspiring book achieves that, and rightfully so. He grew up in difficult times and overcame many obstacles. Knowing him and his accomplishments makes us all want to be better and do better.

I am certain that after reading this historical book, you will agree that we need more people in our world like Robert J. Brown.

—Stedman Graham
New York Times *bestselling author, speaker, and businessman*

YOU CAN'T GO WRONG DOING RIGHT

AN UNEXPECTED VISIT

Pretoria, South Africa, November 1988

A LOUD KNOCK CAME ON THE DOOR OF MY HOTEL ROOM, IN-terrupting my packing. I'd been in South Africa tending to both personal and business matters, and now I was preparing to go home to North Carolina.

I went to the door and looked through the peephole to see who was there. Two large white men, wearing suits, likely from the feared National Intelligence Service of the apartheid government.

I paused before opening the door to my room, weighing my options. These were dangerous times for black men and women in South Africa. Thousands had disappeared under apartheid rule, in which leaders of the white minority marginalized and terrorized the black majority with murders, beatings, bombings, and torture. The racists in the apartheid government were well aware of my friendship with their high-profile prisoner, resistance leader Nelson Mandela; his wife, Winnie; and other anti-apartheid activists.

All of my instincts told me to be wary. My survival skills were well honed—first as a black child growing up under Jim Crow laws in the South, then as a police officer in my hometown and as an undercover federal narcotics agent in New York and other urban areas. They were further developed while I worked alongside the Reverend Martin Luther King Jr. and his civil rights warriors during the violent 1960s, and further still as a special assistant to the president of the United States after that.

Over those years, I'd been slashed with a knife, assaulted, jailed, threatened, and harassed. Yet, South Africa, in that moment, was the most dangerous place I'd ever been. Blacks and whites were engaged in open warfare. There'd been assassinations, kidnappings, car bombings, and mass arrests.

Another knock rattled the door, more insistent this time. I checked the peephole again. The two imposing white men were holding ID cards up for inspection. They were State House identification cards, which meant these National Intelligence Service agents were assigned to the office of the president.

Alarmed, I stepped back.

Should I flee out a window? Call friends for assistance?

I doubted that the NIS security force would brazenly kidnap an American who'd served in the White House, even a black one. Still, in this country, at this time, extreme measures could not be ruled out.

I said a prayer and opened the door.

"Hello, gentlemen. How can I help you?"

Their manner was formal and nonthreatening, but their message was stunning.

"Mr. Brown, President Botha would like to chat with you before you leave the country. We know you plan to leave tomorrow, but we could arrange for you to meet with him this evening."

I hardly knew what to say. South African president P. W. Botha was known then, as he is now, as one of the most evil men of the twentieth century, allegedly responsible for the torture and murder of thousands of blacks, as well as hundreds of bombings and burnings in black townships.

His nickname was *Die Groot Krokodil,* which is Afrikaans for "The Big Crocodile." At that very moment, he was the jailer of my friend Nelson Mandela, who'd been imprisoned for more than twenty years. Botha represented all of the racial hatred I'd known in my life. The thought of being alone in a room with him stirred the rage in me. I silently prayed for God's strength to contain it.

The Afrikaner security officers were waiting for my response to their president's invitation. *Can I trust them? Can I trust myself?*

Then, as has happened throughout my life, I heard the voice of the woman who raised me. My guiding light, my grandmother: Miss Nellie Brown.

Bobby, you never know which way the Lord is coming at you.

Yes, Mama, I'm still listening, I thought.

Then I turned to the two NIS men and gave them my answer: "What time does President Botha wish to see me?"

I WAS RAISED always to ask "How can I help?" You might say it became my calling card.

Some of the earliest memories of my childhood include long days with my grandmother, raising chickens and tending to our home garden. We had no money for groceries most of the time, so our garden was the source of most of our meals—except for what Miss Nellie insisted on giving away.

We canned everything we didn't eat, except for our garden potatoes, which we buried eight inches deep under the front porch and covered in straw because we didn't have a refrigerator. Sweet potatoes on one side, white potatoes on the other. We guarded them for ourselves, until Mama felt someone needed a meal more than we did.

"Bobby, go dig up some potatoes and give them to this man."

Serving others was part of Mama's walk of faith, and it became mine as well. Anytime I strayed in that walk, Miss Nellie's voice put me back on the path. She turned me around time and time again.

Her voice was there throughout my adulthood too. My path took me through vibrant and often violent times. I was jailed and threatened in the civil rights era, sent on missions around the world by the president of the United States, and challenged by authorities for defying apartheid laws in South Africa. Through it all, I came to know a few of the most renowned figures in modern history. This book tells those stories, while also sharing the simple lessons I learned from my grandmother that guided me through a life of many peaks and valleys. Her wise words lifted me up when I felt powerless, and kept me humble at times when I had the power of the presidency behind me.

Mama's mind-set of serving others first was ingrained in me as a way of living. Putting others first also elevated my life and helped me rise above any of my own fear and anger. Instead, I used that energy to do as much good as possible.

I have seen many examples of fear and anger turn into rage. When anyone is consumed by either of those characteristics, they are challenged to find the faith to heal. History has not made a final decision on how to judge Richard M. Nixon yet. To some, he was a tragic historical figure. To others, he was a man with the right experiences and aspirations to lead the world to a better place. I will always remember the many wonderful things that he accomplished and the many opportunities he gave to me and thousands of others.

Two of the other great leaders with whom I shared a path at different times in my life—the Reverend Martin Luther King Jr. and, later, Nelson Mandela—were renowned for deploying their anger and rage into a force that drove them to create powerful social change. Instead of wreaking violence, they wielded forgiveness and fought for healing. Dr. King and Nelson Mandela both followed Jesus's advice to "love your enemies," because they saw the true power in choosing faith over anger.

"There's something about love that builds up and is creative," Martin once said. "There is something about hate that tears down and is destructive. So, love your enemies."

He lived that belief, as did Nelson Mandela, and they moved mountains.

As for me, I stayed mostly in the shadows and did not seek the limelight. My job, as I saw it, was to offer my help wherever it was needed. To work quietly to bring differing people together for a greater good. One of my greatest assets was that I learned to love everyone, even those who did me wrong.

"You can find good anywhere, and you can do good everywhere," Mama would always say.

And after eighty-some years on this Earth, I would say I have to agree.

PART ONE

Chapter 1

YOU DON'T HAVE TO BE RICH TO GIVE

I GREW UP WITH MY BROTHER, BILL, IN MY GRANDPARENTS' house in High Point, North Carolina. We lived in Burns Hill, one of the poorest of the colored neighborhoods in town. White folks had homes along paved streets. Blacks lived where the pavement ended. Our humble wood-frame bungalow was located at 1309 East Commerce Street, where there was neither commerce nor a street.

The Hill was mostly peaceful in my 1940s boyhood, but it was not a place that inspired much hope. Families were from the working poor. Most scraped by on skimpy earnings, but they took care of each other, sharing what little they had because serving others was how we all survived.

One day when I was not yet ten years old, a man reeking of sour wine and wet garbage walked up to our porch. I was sitting on our house's wooden front steps, and my "Mama," my grandmother, was in her chair on the porch. The man stood at the bottom of the steps, unsteady on his feet and red-eyed, but cautious and respectful.

"I ain't had nothin' to eat for two days, Miss Nellie," he said. "I don't have no money to buy food."

I stood up, suspicious of the beggar and protective of my grandmother. But Mama had no fear of him.

"Come on in here, boy," she said to the man.

He climbed the stairs with surprising speed, followed her into the house, and took a seat at the kitchen table. Mama went right to work. She broke off chunks from a huge pan of homemade bread and dished up a bowl of hot beans. The man ate until his belly stopped growling. Then he let fly a roaring belch, stood up from the table, gently placed his bowl in the sink, and said: "I sure do appreciate it, Miss Nellie. The Lord will bless you."

Mama turned from the sink and sighed. The man had to know he was in for one of her church lectures, but no doubt he'd figured the meal would be worth it.

"Do the right thing, now, and get your life straight," Mama told him, looking him in the eye. "Go to church on Sunday and your life will change for the better."

He bowed his head, accepting his penance, and then made his way out the door and down the steps with newfound energy. Mama washed his bowl and returned to her chair on the porch. I took my place on the steps. After a while, I gathered the courage to say what was on my mind.

"Mama, why on earth do you give our food to these people who spend their days and nights drinkin' and sleepin' in the street, when you and Daddy and Bill and me work so hard to put it on the table?"

My question must have touched something in her. Mama waved for me to come up and sit in the chair with her. When I'd settled in, she told me a story from the Bible, of the time when Jesus knocked on someone's door for help, but they turned Him away because He was dressed in rags.

"If I never teach you anything else," she said, "I want to teach you that one thing—you never know which way the Lord will come to you. He will test you to see if you follow His teachings. So, life is all about giving, sharing, and serving others. If you give whatever you can, the Lord will give you more than you will ever need. He will take you up so high you won't believe it."

Mama was wound up. I listened as a life's worth of lessons poured out of her.

"Son, you don't have to be rich to give. We aren't rich, but we had food in the pot today. The Lord provided that food, and he provided it to me so I could share it with others. He gave us enough to share. That's what you should do with your life, Bobby. Whatever you get, make sure you try to help somebody else with it, because the Lord gives it to you so you can give it to somebody else."

MISS NELLIE BROWN was the light that woke me up in the morning and put me to bed at night. I adored her and took her words as gospel to live by. She had so much wisdom, so much compassion. Or, as Martin Luther King Jr. once said, "a heart full of grace and a soul generated by love."

My grandmother took in my brother and me shortly after we arrived in this world. Our natural birth mother, Gracie Mae Marshall, ran away from home early in her teens, and we were never clear on how she survived during those years. She'd been sixteen when Bill was born, and I arrived two years later, on February 26, 1935. For most of my childhood, Gracie Mae was like an older sister or cousin who rarely came around.

We called our grandparents "Mama" and "Daddy," throughout our lives. My grandfather, Marcus Lafayette Brown, worked in the boiler room of one of High Point's many furniture factories. A quiet and humble man by nature, he usually worked late shifts, so he left most of the grandchild-rearing to our grandmother. I felt blessed to have them as my parents, and couldn't have loved them more.

Before we complicated her life, Mama had worked full-time at the Southern Railway station in High Point. She cleaned the station and called the trains, shouting out arrival and departure times for all to hear. Mama was well known at church and at the railway station for her booming voice. Some claimed they could hear Mama's train calls five stops up and five stops down the line.

She had the same reach when calling us home from our ball

fields, creek explorations, and friends' homes. You could be six blocks away and underwater and still hear Miss Nellie calling us home to supper.

"Billeeeeeeeeeee! Bobbeeeeee! Time for dinnahhhhhh, boys!"

We scooted, too. Even the other kids listened to Mama. She had this air of authority that said, *There will be no shady business when I'm around.*

Mama was an imposing woman. Big-boned and straight-backed, she had a regal bearing, no matter that she wore thrift shop dresses sometimes held together with safety pins. Whether singing in our church's gospel choir or canning vegetables, she called out Jesus with the best of them, and she set our moral compasses with lessons from the Bible.

The power and clarity of her voice certainly carried me a long way. Whenever my anger threatened to explode, her lessons of faith would come to me and help me redirect the rage toward positive action. I could well have ended up in prison, or worse, if it were not for all the Godly messages my Mama put in my heart as I was growing up.

BY MOST EXPECTATIONS, I wasn't ever supposed to get off the Hill. In fact, there were times when it looked like I wouldn't make it past childhood at all. I coughed and wheezed throughout most days, and on two or three occasions, these fits led to pneumonia and weeks of confinement to my bed. Today, I know the coughing came from asthma, but back then, black children who coughed and wheezed weren't taken to the doctor. We were just considered poor and frail.

I was so skinny and pale, the other kids called me "Light Bread." The nickname dogged me through elementary school. Since I lacked physical strength, I learned to get along through gentle persuasion and negotiation. The role of peacemaker suited me. If another boy got mad because he didn't have enough marbles, I'd give him some of mine. I wanted everybody to be happy. When kids couldn't agree on whether to play baseball or go swimming, they left it up to me to decide. It's funny how our childhood ways offer previews into our adult lives.

To be truthful, I also had a childhood bodyguard who protected me from bullies as well as snakes and other dangers. My older brother, Bill, was nicknamed the "Brown Bomber" from early childhood. Bill was stump-necked, thick-shouldered, and fast with his fists. Later in his Air Force career, he became the middleweight champ of the Fifth Division. No one messed with Bill.

My brother and I spent at least part of every day in the garden, busting our butts to raise vegetables and fruit. While other kids in our neighborhood were playing stickball or hanging out, we had to hoe, weed, and pick. Mama had a knack for drawing spiritual and life lessons out of everyday experiences, especially gardening. Every spring, we'd go to Hauser's farm goods and garden store on Wrenn Street to buy seeds and fertilizer for the garden. Mama always made sure we bought two or three pounds of black mustard seed, which came in a brown paper sack.

The first time I went with her, I thought she'd bought too much.

"What do you plan to do with all those little-bitty seeds?" I asked.

Mama jumped right on that question as if she'd been waiting for it. She reached into the sack, pulled out a small handful of the tiny dark black seeds, and opened her palm to display them.

"Bobby," she said, "even if your faith is no bigger than a grain of this seed, it will help you move mountains one day."

I still didn't know why she'd bought so many of those seeds. But I found that lesson inspiring long before I knew Mama was quoting the Bible. I figured she was just making it up. Imagine my surprise when I went to Sunday school and found the parable of the mustard seed mentioned several times in the Gospels. Before I knew better, I thought maybe Mama had shared her story with its authors.

This was not a big leap, because Miss Nellie was a sort of high priestess in the church of our upbringing. Her father had been lay pastor of the Sneedsboro African Methodist Episcopal Zion Church near Wadesboro—a church that my great-grandfather, a former slave, had built in the 1880s.

Each year, Mama headed up a benefit dinner for the church, with fried fish and homemade ice cream prepared by members. The congregation used the funds to make repairs on the church Mama's father had built. Bill and I would ride the 100 miles with her on a Trailways bus and then help paint and patch the old brick building and its crumbling foundation. So much of its mortar had turned to dust that I feared it would collapse someday when the choir roared through one of its mighty crescendos.

Bill and I were baptized in High Point's own St. Stephen AME Zion Church. Church was our sanctuary in a separate and unequal world, the one place where we could sing, praise God, and let our hair down without having to worry about being accused or judged or looked down upon. Social connections, business connections, and spiritual connections were forged there.

Nearly every week, we took our prayer books on the road with Mama, who was in great demand as the leader and star performer of the Heavenly Gospel Choir. She and the choir traveled all over North Carolina and Virginia in a ragged old bus that was maintained by roadside mechanics across both states. Some Sundays, she would sing in front of three or four congregations.

Mama was a gospel diva. All eyes would leave the prayer books when Nellie Brown came marching down the aisle, her head held high and her Sunday finery swishing.

Preachers would interrupt their own sermons when they spied Mama making her entrance. "We are blessed on this great day, because Miss Nellie Brown is here! I'm hopeful that she will grace us with a selection from her songbook before the service is over."

Meanwhile, my brother and I would trail behind in our neckties and knickers, feeling special in Mama's glow. She was in her glory as she sang, shooing the pigeons from the bell tower with her powerful, deep contralto.

Mama led a simple home life, cooking and cleaning and caring for her handed-back grand-boys. Singing was her release and her reward, as well as her private line to the Heavenly Father. That choir, and the African Methodist Episcopal Zion Church, filled all the empty and dark corners of her life, and I think she wanted it to do the same for us.

There was another person who drove my ambitions in those early days, and for many decades beyond. Her name was Sallie Walker. Her family did not live on Burns Hill, and they belonged to a different church that I attended only because my grandmother was a guest soloist in the gospel choir.

On one of these church visits with Mama, I spied Sallie watching me over the top of her family's front-row pew. She was always dressed so pretty, big brown eyes, curly black hair, and a smile that made me trip over my own feet. We were five or six years old, neither of us in school yet, so all I could do was look at her from across the church. Even after school started, it remained a me-watching-her-watching-me sort of relationship for a couple of years. By the time we entered the third grade, I worked up the courage to actually speak to her. I was shy and reserved. She was Sallie. Bold and beautiful.

Sallie's family was high society compared to ours. She lived in a nice house with running water, central heat, and a television, too. Downing Street was a few blocks above Burns Hill. Her daddy was a hustler, and I mean that in the best sense. He was a kindhearted and generous man who had many friends and, always, a lot of jobs.

He built rental houses all over Greensboro and High Point, but his main job was managing the local Elks Club. Blacks weren't allowed to join it, or drink in it, but George Walker had the keys to the biggest liquor cabinet in our town. He had clout in our community. People came to him for jobs and loans as well as liquor. Everyone looked up to him as an "enterprising man." I didn't even know the term back then, but he served as an early role model for me: self-made, confident enough to work on both sides of town.

George Walker ran a more formal household than my own. His daughter Sallie called me "Robert" from the start, never "Bob." She seemed to take me more seriously than I took myself. We shared a love of reading and a hunger to experience the world outside High Point. On our long walks to and from school, she shared her dreams of one day living in a big city and going to museums, concerts, and plays. All of that seemed like fantasy to me, but from our earliest times together, I found myself trying to rise to her expectations.

Sallie liked that I listened well, because she often needed to vent about her family. Her parents had an on-again, off-again marriage. They divorced, remarried, and divorced again before we'd graduated from junior high school. Despite their rocky relationship, Sallie enjoyed a higher level of comfort and security than most black children in our town.

In the fifth or sixth grade, we made our relationship official and became boyfriend and girlfriend. I was infatuated to the point of self-endangerment. I couldn't sleep at night if I didn't see Sallie. I'd sing songs to her, and even write poems to her.

She sat at the front of our class because she was so smart, which motivated me to work hard so I could be up there by her. Her early impressions of me were not the stuff of romance novels. She said I was "mature and sensible." I had hoped for something more heroic, but I took what I could get.

———

IN THOSE DAYS, most black families in the South were just an ancestor or two removed from the great burden of slavery. My grandmother's father, Joseph Kendall, had been among the millions of men and women who were bought and sold and treated like livestock. The emotions attached to that aspect of our family history are complex, to say the least. They certainly impacted me in ways I will never fully understand.

I do know that I drew from a deep well of strength. My maternal great-grandfather, and so many others in my lineage, had endured torments unimaginable to me. They were forced to work until they could not stand up. They were beaten if they went down. They were not allowed to own property, or to attend schools. Their families were torn apart. They had no choice in where they lived. They saw friends and family members tortured, burned, hung from trees, and dragged through the streets.

Yet they persevered.

As hard as I might think life was for me and my family sometimes, our lives were so much easier than those of previous generations. Mama often told us that, as we were growing up. We learned to shoulder our burdens with grace, and to put our lives in God's hands.

We were raised in faith, but rage was part of our inheritance too. I first felt its burn when Mama told us her father was often whipped with a strap by his "masters." Her father would gather Mama and her siblings around the fireplace and tell them stories from his slave days. He said that in the late 1800s, when he was a young man, his owners would rent him and other slaves out to the builders of the North Carolina Railroad. They'd send horse-drawn wagons to haul them to the construction sites, where they'd often work for weeks at a time. As an adult, I learned that the builders of the North Carolina Railroad were known to treat slaves so badly that many owners refused to let their slaves work on it, for fear of losing them.

My great-grandfather was eventually freed and became a farmer, raising cotton and vegetables. Mama, born in 1892, was the second oldest of his ten girls and one boy. They lived in an unpainted wood-frame house with a huge stone fireplace used for cooking and heat. Several of her sisters were still living when I was a child. Mama would take us to visit them on their small farms, and they always sent us home with bags of vegetables and cured hog meat.

When my grandmother deemed us old enough, she took us a little deeper into our family history. This time the bus stopped in Fayetteville, North Carolina, for a layover of several hours. As we stepped off the bus, I thought of Mama's stories, filling my mind with visions of what this town must have looked like in my great-grandfather's slave days. Instead of the street lined with cars, I imagined mule-drawn wagons rumbling along dirt roads, and my grandfather dressed in raggedy clothes, jostling with other black boys and men packed into the wagon bed.

My thoughts were interrupted when Mama stopped a man on the sidewalk and asked: "Where is the old slave market?"

He directed her down the street for a block or two, to the "big ol' building," pointing to a third-story clock tower above the tree line in the distance.

My grandmother then turned to Bill and me and said, "I want to show you where my father was sold for the last time."

I'll never forget that moment. She walked us to what is now a historic landmark known as the Market House, but to us it was always called "the old slave market"; it was the place where my great-grandfather and thousands of other black men, women, and children were auctioned off and sold. Like they were less than human beings.

"This is the last place where my father was sold as a slave," she said once more.

I've never let go of the image of my great-grandfather chained and on the block for bidders. It was sealed in my mind. Whenever

I think of it, I first feel this deep sadness like a sharp pain in my heart, and then anger boils up in me. My cheeks flush and the veins in my head start to throb.

Some days, I wake up with that anger. Some nights, I go to bed with it. Haunted by images of my great-grandfather being whipped. Memories of racism and injustice I've endured in my own time. Over the years, that anger has given my life direction and driven me to champion other victims. On more than one occasion, it undoubtedly has saved my life. Knowing it is there can be a source of concern, because anger can consume you if you're not careful. But it is also true that having that anger within me can be a comfort, and a source of security—like having a knife to pull out if I need it.

Mama talked about her father more after that visit. It was as if she'd introduced us to him and thereafter felt like we knew him too. He had died in 1912 after a life spent in slavery and poverty, but despite his difficult life, my grandmother remembered him as a man with a hopeful vision for the future.

"He would say, 'Watch and wait. Man is getting wiser. There will be men flying in the air and riding on machines,'" Mama told me. "He had a lot of wisdom, Bobby, and I think some of that passed on to you."

NEARLY A CENTURY after the state's slave markets closed, High Point was not without its racial problems. I grew up in a neighborhood where we were shielded from the most overt remnants, but once we roamed off our dirt roads and onto the paved streets of the white neighborhoods, there were always reminders.

My first trips with Mama downtown were eye-opening, especially when we went to the Woolworth's store. The heavenly smells from the lunch counter and the candy section were almost more than I could handle, but I was puzzled by the signs on the two water fountains at the back.

One was marked WHITE WATER. The other said COLORED WATER.

I asked Mama what the difference was. She said we weren't supposed to drink the "white water."

"Does it taste any different?" I asked.

"It all comes from the same place," she replied. "The white folks just want their own place to drink from."

I found this confusing. When we played ball against the white kids, there was never any talk of them using different balls, bats, or bases. It must have been an adult thing.

Downtown had other pitfalls for us. We were about seven or eight years old when my best boyhood friend, James Jett, told me about a run-in he'd had with a white man there. His aunt had taken him downtown to get some clothing for school. Jett had just received a real short haircut, and I guess the temptation was too much for one of the white clothing salesmen. "You're a real cute little fellow," he said. "I need some luck, let me rub your head."

The white man had no way of knowing that black children were very superstitious about letting someone rub our heads. As the legend went, the person who rubbed your head would get all your good luck and you'd be left with nothing but bad luck. So, when the white guy knuckled his head, Jett kicked him hard in the shins to hold on to his good luck.

Jett's poor aunt nearly fainted at the sight of him bruising the shin of that salesman. She snatched him up and hauled him out of that store before the guy had time to retaliate.

After they put some distance between themselves and the store, Jett's aunt wagged a finger at him and warned: "Don't you ever kick a white man again."

Jett took his aunt's warning to heart, but later he shared his deepest fear with me.

"He took all my luck," he said, with tears rolling from his eyes.

Jett wasn't afraid of that man, but his aunt's reaction worried him. He'd never seen her so frightened. I didn't really understand the depth of that fear until I began reading the black newspapers that were passed around from family to family on Burns Hill.

As a child, I was a hungry reader, always wanting to know about the world. A neighbor lady, Mrs. Lytle, did cleaning for some wealthy white families downtown, and she'd bring me brown bags packed with magazines and city newspapers they'd thrown out. I was thrilled to get the white people's *Time, Life,* and *National Geographic* magazines. I'd read them until I fell asleep at home.

But the stories and photographs in the *Baltimore Afro-American* and the *New Journal and Guide* had a different effect on me. The Negro press, as it was known then, carried stories and pictures of lynchings that were taking place even as I was growing up. They had graphic photographs of black men and women hanging in trees from ropes around their necks. The images haunted me then, and they have stayed with me throughout my life, asleep or awake.

My fear of racists grew stronger year by year. My friends and I often shared stories about people being hauled off, beaten, or killed by whites for no real reason other than being black. Bill and I made some good money cutting grass with an old push mower, but we were on edge whenever we knocked on the doors of whites to ask for work or payment. I was afraid to look them in the eyes, especially white women. I always turned away for fear of being accused of one thing or another.

This was not an unreasonable fear. I was still a young man in 1955 when Emmett Till was beaten, shot, and hanged for allegedly saying "Bye, baby" to a white woman in a store while visiting family in Mississippi. The black newspapers kept a running count that we checked on a regular basis. It was open season on our people.

Since those days, I've spent a good part of my life—more than a half century—fighting racial hatred, discrimination, and fear. I've seen substantial changes in government policy, some of which I had a hand in. Blacks have access to opportunity like never before, and yet racism is still a threat, a daily threat for most.

That is why those newspaper photographs of lynchings still haunt me. These horrible visions visited me when I traveled with Martin Luther King Jr. in the 1960s, when I walked across the White House lawn, and while driving through Africa to meet with the Mandela family. Even now, when I see a tree with a limb hanging out parallel to the ground, I can't block the image of a black figure hanging from it.

This happens in my most serene moments and in the most secure places; whether playing golf at Augusta National or visiting with friends at a cocktail party. I can be anywhere in the world, but if I see a big old tree with sweeping low limbs, the first thing that comes into my mind is those images of "strange fruit."

Sallie, who knew my mind all too well, was once with me on vacation at Sea Island, Georgia, when she saw me staring at a big tree.

"Leave it alone, Robert," she said.

I only wish I could.

This haunting is a curse, without a doubt, yet it also serves as a constant reminder to stay alert, and to keep the struggle alive.

Chapter 2

THE LORD DOESN'T MAKE MISTAKES

FOR THE MOST PART, I WAS A HAPPY BOY. OUR FAMILY WASN'T poor and suffering. Just poor. Our clothes were homemade or bought secondhand at the Catholic Thrift Shop. We stuck bits of cardboard into our shoes so we could keep wearing them even after the soles wore out. Sometimes my grandfather would patch those holes with worn-out leather belts from his wood lathe machine at work. Daddy's homemade insoles worked as well as any from Dr. Scholl's.

Our grandparents took us in at a time when they should have been slowing down and taking life a little easier. Bill and I realized this more and more as we got closer to our teens. We didn't want to be a burden on them, so we tried to pitch in by finding work where we could. My buddy Jett says one of his most vivid memories from our shared boyhood is looking up from the ball field to the hill above it and seeing me, shoe-shine box in hand, trudging toward downtown to make a few dollars while the rest of the kids were playing baseball.

Most of my moneymaking opportunities were along High Point's rowdy Washington Street, home to bars, restaurants, shops, and the Ritz Theater—the only movie house where black folks weren't forced to sit in the balcony.

On Friday afternoons and Saturdays, Bill and I polished the beer stains and mud off dress shoes. Our customers were white guys from the pool halls and taverns who'd just cashed their paychecks and were sprucing up for a night on the town. They'd step out on the street and yell, "Hey boy! I need a shine!" On more than a few occasions, they'd call me "nigger."

Sometimes a customer who was drunk, or just mean, would kick me or spit on me as I sat at his feet. I didn't complain. You didn't do that if you needed the work. Instead, I'd snap to it and hope I'd end up with a tip.

The charge was fifteen cents to a quarter for a shine. We'd work until dark and leave downtown with as many coins as our pockets could hold. By the time we reached high school age, Bill and I had worked our way up to a brick-and-mortar location, the High Point Hat Shop, where my uncle had shined shoes as a high school student.

The Hat Shop was a big step up from working on the streets with a shine box. It had ten chairs with brass footrests. Greek businessman Phillip Melonas owned the shop, but John Akers ran it and he was a master at his craft.

John taught us to dampen our cloths so we could work up a glassy finish on the shoe after applying our polish. A showman by nature, he also taught us how to make our buff rags pop and crack as we worked, adding some entertainment flash to the routine. Thanks to Mr. Akers's tutoring, we began taking in $30 and $50 a day on weekends, and even more during "market weeks" when High Point's furniture showrooms filled with shoppers from all over the country.

If things were slow downtown in the dog days of summer, Bill and I worked as caddies at the whites-only Emerywood Country Club. I became an avid golfer later in life, but it took me a long time to get over the racism I encountered at the High Point course. Some members there made the black caddies line up in the mornings, and they'd pick over us like plantation owners examining livestock.

"I'll take that niggah boy there. C'mon, caddy, get your black ass up here!"

"Let's get that boy over there, he looks like a good nigger."

"He looks like a good racehorse."

I was thin, and it bothered me to no end when the white men judged me to be too skinny to carry their clubs. I took their money, but I burned at their racist taunts. I could only take so much of it, so after a while I caddied only when I couldn't make a buck somewhere else.

When I'd go home and tell my grandmother about being cursed and mocked and called "nigger" by white people, she told me to use their cruel words as motivation to study hard in school, so I could follow my God-given purpose.

"Always remember, son, you are not a problem. You are a prize," she'd say. "The Lord doesn't make mistakes."

BY MY JUNIOR YEAR at William Penn High School, my asthma had begun to subside. I wanted to play football, so I signed up for the team tryouts. My friends were not encouraging.

"Light Bread, you're gonna be toast out there!"

By then, I'd grown to about six feet in height and added some rangy muscle, but my body was still sliced pretty thin. I didn't match up well against the beefiest guys, so my main contribution during most games was keeping the bench warm for the starters. As the season progressed, it seemed like the only way I'd see the field was if a sudden outbreak of the flu hospitalized the entire first team.

Then, in the second-to-last game of the season, we played Thomasville High and their star defensive tackle, Cement Sam. He wasn't particularly tall, but he was thick as a cellblock wall and deceptively quick off the ball. From the start of the game he went through our offensive line like it was a paper chain, blowing past all the blockers and creaming our quarterback.

To add insult to injury, Sam spit on my teammates between plays and threw clods of dirt into their faces. Whimpers arose from our sidelines, infuriating our coach.

"Isn't there SOMEBODY who can block that guy? Anybody?"
he yelled. Then he said something even more alarming—at least for
my teammates.

"Brown, get out there!"

Coach had already thrown all of his starters and most of the
second string at Sam. I guess he decided it couldn't hurt to send
me out there. Maybe Sam would trip over me and break an ankle.

Our quarterback, Alfonso Charles, did a double-take when he
saw me trotting up. "Coach sent YOU? You can't block nobody!
That guy is going to punch a hole in you, Light Bread!"

Naturally, Alfonso threw me to the lions right away, calling a
play that sent a running back through my spot on the line. I was
supposed to clear out Cement Sam. When the ball was snapped, I
threw all I had at the little sucker.

Sam didn't know what hit him, because *nothing* hit him. He
dodged my attempt to spear him, grabbed my shoulder pad, and
threw me to the ground like a dirty handkerchief. He then did a
tap dance across my spine on his way to demolishing the halfback.

It wasn't the heroic debut I'd envisioned, but I became determined that this stumpy guy wasn't going to end my football career
before it started. In the huddle, I told Alfonso to run the same play.

"I'm gonna nail him this time," I said.

There weren't any *amen*s in response. Nobody in the huddle
said a word. They didn't believe me.

When Sam lined up across from me before the next play, I
didn't let on that I was mad enough to gnaw off his spikes. Instead,
I put on a meek act and lined up as far back as possible, like I was
afraid to take him on.

Sam reeked of confidence, flaring his nostrils and flexing his bi-
ceps. He looked like he was preparing to drop-kick my helmet into
the end zone, with my head still in it. When the ball was snapped,
he charged in my direction as if I didn't exist.

What Sam didn't realize was that I'd taken a couple steps back from the line of scrimmage not because I was afraid of him, but so I could make a run at him, too.

As he flew across the line, I crouched low and made myself a missile aimed at his rib cage. He hadn't expected any resistance, so when my helmet hammered his gut, Sam folded like a two-dollar tent. I landed on top of him and tried to grind him into powder. Our halfback looked so surprised to see me on top of Sam, I thought he was going to stop and congratulate me. Instead, he just smiled as he scooted by for a ten-yard gain.

When the play was over, Sam had to be helped off the field. I don't think he was in pain. I'm certain he was in shock—and to be honest, so was I. This aggressive side of me was something new. I liked it, and so did my coach. I started at left tackle for the last two games of the season. My goal was to give my opponent a whupping on every play.

I'd always thought of my brother as the tough guy in the family, so my confidence grew with my success on the football field. I was starting to mature and fill out in other ways, too. My grades had improved, and I had also been named class president and editor of the school newspaper, *The Student's Penn*. Sallie worked as my top assistant editor, though at one point she nearly left me over a typo. Somehow I had failed to notice that her name was misspelled in a story. Decades later, it would still come up from time to time. Sallie didn't play around.

My final editorial for the high school paper was titled "Facing the Future Unafraid," and the conclusion reflected my newfound self-confidence, as well as the influence of my grandmother's teachings.

"Endeavor yourselves to work hard and be prepared," I wrote. *"Hitch your wagon to a star and never stop striving for your goal."*

My efforts to write an inspiring editorial may not have been

Pulitzer-worthy, but looking back, I can see that they were words I chose to live by. The young man standing at the gateway was me. Somewhere deep inside, I was deciding what I wanted to achieve in life and how I would claim it.

College had always been a goal of mine, but as my senior year approached I didn't see how I could continue my education. The costs were too daunting for a Burns Hill boy. I did not want to add to my grandparents' burden, even though they encouraged me to pursue a college degree somehow.

I had the grades and the determination, but not the funds. Still, I studied and read so much that my classmates ridiculed me: "Light Bread man, you tryin' to be smarter than everybody else?"

The answer to that was *Yes*. I'd been on a mission to prove that I wasn't a "slow" student since my first year in grade school, when the teacher held me back because I'd had so many sick days. Instead of being promoted to second grade at the end of that first year, I was put in a "high" first-grade class, meant for low-achieving students whose teachers felt weren't prepared to advance.

I was devastated. Mama tried to console me. "It's okay, Bobby, you'll do fine, just let it go. If you just keep working and studying hard, you'll make it." But I couldn't shake the feeling that I'd let her down.

I believe my determined push out of poverty began right there. It wasn't that I wanted to be wealthy; I just wanted to make Mama and Daddy proud. Sallie was another positive influence in that regard (and most others). She was always one of the smartest students in our school, and she stayed on my case every day to raise my grades. She studied with me and helped me prepare for tests.

If I didn't get A's, there was hell to pay, because Sallie's report card never had anything lower. Sallie had always planned to attend college, and her parents could afford to send her. My path was not so clear. I even considered following a couple friends into the Air

Force, until my high school principal, Mr. Sam Burford, told me that it would be "tragic" if I didn't at least give college a try.

The next thing I knew, he'd pulled a few strings and secured athletic and academic scholarships for me at his alma mater, Virginia Union University in Richmond, one of the oldest black universities in the nation. I enrolled with the freshman class in 1954, as a history major intending to play defensive end on the football team.

In those days, freshmen weren't allowed to play with the varsity, so I threw myself into my studies that first year. I was intent on making the most of my class time, because even with my double scholarship, the living costs were a heavy burden for my grandparents. I felt responsible to do my best since they were supporting my education. Things were especially lean since Bill had been drafted and sent to Korea, so he was no longer able to help them out at home.

My grandparents were on their own, and not in the best health. Marcus had diabetes. He could hardly walk because of the poor circulation in his legs and feet. My grandmother suffered from arthritis and high blood pressure. Neither of them could get around much. I worried about them constantly.

Sallie was also on my mind. She had enrolled at Hampton University on the shore of Chesapeake Bay in Hampton, Virginia, about sixty miles from my school. We visited each other on weekends as often as we could, but most of the time we hit the books to keep up with our classes.

I had top marks that first year, but it was all for naught. I realized my grandparents, who had always refused to go on welfare, would not survive without my assistance. In the spring of 1955, I decided to move back to High Point to live with them and support them. Sallie was disappointed, but she understood that I had a responsibility to help those who had helped me for so long.

At the end of the semester, we met in Richmond. We wanted to ride the train back to High Point, but I had no money. I had to pawn Sallie's portable typewriter to pay for my ticket.

I never got that typewriter back. Sallie would remind me of that quite often over the years.

AFTER MOVING BACK in with my grandparents, I worked here and there doing part-time jobs. I also enrolled at North Carolina Agricultural and Technical State University in Greensboro, hoping to continue my studies part-time. With no car to drive, I hitchhiked to classes most days.

My continuing education ended after about a year, though, when a police detective came knocking at my grandparents' house one day. I was gone at the time, so Mama answered the door. The High Point officer identified himself as Detective Captain Johnson and asked for me.

"Bobby isn't home, is he in trouble for something?"

The detective gave her a strange smile and handed her his business card.

"Just have him call me, please?"

You can imagine her concern.

"Are you in some kind of trouble, Bobby?" Miss Nellie asked as I walked in the front door. I'd never seen such a worried expression on her face.

"What's going on?" I said.

"The police are looking for you," she said. "A detective came by this morning and left this card. Later, the neighbors told me he'd called them to ask about you. He wanted to know what kind of person you were."

I had no idea what the detective might have wanted. I told her that I'd done nothing wrong.

"Well, you are supposed to call the police department right away and ask for him."

We had no phone in the house, so I went across the street to Mrs. Dunlap's and used hers. Captain Johnson, a white fellow, answered.

"Oh yes, Robert, I just want to talk to you a bit. Will you be home in the next half hour? I'll stop by."

He offered no reason for his visit, but he seemed in a hurry to see me. Now I was worried too.

"They aren't going to take you away, are they?" Mama asked.

She had cause for concern. In those days, it wasn't at all unusual for someone from my neighborhood to be blindsided by an anonymous accusation. People would get arrested and hauled off to jail for a burglary, a car theft, or even on a rape charge because they fit the vague description of "a young black male."

The possibility weighed on my mind, so by the time Detective Johnson and another white officer walked up to our front porch, I was a wreck. Their first question did nothing to ease my anxiety.

"You took the police officer's exam a while back, didn't you?" the detective asked.

I'd completely forgotten about that. In the spring of 1956, I'd taken a sociology course at NCA&T dealing with law enforcement and its impact on society. One week, while researching a class assignment on the role of policemen in the community, I found an ad in the High Point newspaper that said the city was testing applicants for the local police department. I thought it might help my grade if I took the exam and wrote about the experience, so I took the test a few days later. It didn't seem particularly hard, but then again, I wasn't under any pressure. This was just research for my class—or so I thought.

I wrote my paper about taking the police department application exam, and my professor awarded me an A. But I hadn't thought about the application again until the two detectives showed up at our door. I was in such a state of shock and fear, I blurted out: "I took the exam, but it wasn't a prank, I swear."

"Well, no, we didn't think you did it as a prank. Especially after I saw your score," Detective Johnson said with a chuckle.

"My score?"

"Yes, Robert, you scored one of the highest marks that anyone has ever had on that test. We'd like you to think about joining our department as a police officer."

Oh Lord. I was stunned. Relieved that I was not in trouble, but still stunned. I'd had no desire to be a police officer. It had never really entered my mind. I didn't know what to say to Detective Johnson other than I'd think it over. Then I thanked him, and he and his partner departed.

I went into the house and told my grandparents what had transpired. Mama still had concerns.

"Are you sure you ain't in no trouble?"

Mama wasn't thrilled about the development. She wanted me to finish college. But Detective Johnson had said I could attend school part-time while working for the department. My grandfather noted that being a city policeman was not a bad job for a young man without many opportunities.

However, there were other factors to weigh before taking this unplanned detour from college. At the time, a handful of black men already worked on the High Point police force, but they were allowed to patrol only in Burns Hill and other black neighborhoods. Black police officers did not patrol white neighborhoods, and they did not arrest white people. There was no written regulation with that restriction; that's just how it was.

High Point was no different from most small Southern towns in that regard. Racism and discrimination were such a part of life, you'd go along to get along. I never thought about causing a stir by trying to eat at a whites-only restaurant any more than I'd run a red light or refuse to pay for my groceries.

That's how things had always been, but it was also true that my generation was starting to push for change. The grandsons and granddaughters of slaves felt constricted by Jim Crow laws and the lack of opportunities. Increasingly, they were channeling their frustration into action.

The *Brown v. Board of Education of Topeka* decision, delivered two years earlier, had kindled a flame. The family of a black child named Linda Brown sued her Kansas school board because its members wouldn't allow her to attend the whites-only public school four blocks from her house. Her case went all the way to the U.S. Supreme Court, which ruled in 1954 that public schools could not be segregated.

It would take a year or two before blacks actually dared to test the Court's ruling by enrolling in white public schools. There was no small danger to that undertaking. Jim Crow laws still banned blacks from many public places, and our people were still being lynched and beaten by white mobs if they defied the status quo.

The first significant test of the *Brown* decision occurred a year and a half later, 475 miles to the southwest of High Point. In December 1955, black church leaders in Montgomery, Alabama, had rallied their congregations behind a woman named Rosa Parks, after she was arrested for refusing to give up her bus seat in the blacks section to a white person.

The black community's defiance was met with outrage and violence from foes of desegregation. Whites firebombed the home of the Reverend Martin Luther King Jr., who had moved to Montgomery from Atlanta to lead a boycott of the Montgomery bus system.

Anyone who read the newspapers could tell that there were going to be troubled times ahead. Many of my friends questioned why I would even consider putting on a police uniform. Did I want to be put in the middle of the conflict as a black man in police blue?

Sallie, as usual, had her own critical take on my situation. "Robert, you can be so much more than a policeman," she said. Her fear was that I'd get boxed in and settle for too little from life. She wanted me to reach higher.

Starting pay for a High Point city police officer was $2,640 a year. Money went further back then, but even so, the pay wasn't much. Especially since Sallie and I were hoping to buy our own house one day. I took the job and told her that it was just a step toward something better, though I had no idea what that might be.

Sallie had a stake in my future because she was about to become my wife. On September 15, 1956, we were married at my boyhood church, St. Stephen AME Zion Church in High Point, which remains my church today. There were about forty people, including my grandparents and my birth mother.

My brother, Bill, was serving in Korea at the time, so my newly assigned patrol partner, Lawrence Graves, stood in as best man. We had to work the late shift the next day, so Sallie and I had a one-night honeymoon in Greensboro, just fifteen miles away. To get there, I borrowed a nice little Pontiac convertible from Sallie's aunt.

We stayed at the Magnolia House, which is known as "the house that soul built" because it was the only hotel that welcomed blacks between North Carolina and Virginia during the segregation years. The day after our honeymoon, we returned and, before my shift started, moved our few belongings into Sallie's mother's place, because we couldn't yet afford our own.

Chapter 3

PROTECT AND SERVE

C OOT WAS MY FIRST TEST.
    High Point was such a small town, I knew when I joined the police force that it wouldn't be long before I ran up against someone who'd known me since childhood and refused to respect that ol' Light Bread now had a lawman's badge.

I figured it would probably be an ornery old guy, and I figured right. Just a few weeks on the job, I was driving on night patrol one night with my partner, Officer Graves, when our radio dispatcher told us to check out reports of gunfire on Hoover Street.

We found Andrew "Coot" Mack holding a gun and looking belligerent.

"Coot, what are you doing raising hell? Put that gun down," I said.

Coot didn't put the gun down, which meant I had every right to shoot him, but I didn't. I knew Coot and he knew me.

"Bobby Brown, is that you?" Coot said. "I heard you was a big *po-leese-man* now. Hard to figure, though." He still didn't lower his gun, and neither did I.

Graves and I both had a bead on his heart, but neither of us was inclined to shoot Coot.

I'd known him since our school days. He was a classmate. He'd always been a blustering bully, but he wasn't really that tough. He usually backed down if someone called his bluff.

My police training didn't leave room for compromise in such situations. If someone pointed a gun at you and didn't lower it when you ordered them to, the procedure was clear: Shoot to kill. If I hadn't known Coot so well, I probably would have followed that protocol. Hell, if he hadn't known me since we were kids, he probably would have shot me too.

As it was, Coot just got tired of holding that gun on me. When he lowered it, Graves came up from behind and handcuffed him. That was the end of our confrontation, though it played out in much more dramatic fashion for many weeks and months afterward in coffee shops and honky-tonks all over town.

While there were a few old-timers from the neighborhood who questioned as to why I'd want to arrest ol' Coot, a good number noted that I probably should have shot him the second he pointed a gun at me. Some suggested that I was too soft, or too nice a fella to be a policeman. I probably heard that a thousand times in my days as a High Point cop.

Black officers were paid less than white officers, of course. There were eight of us on the force, two detectives and six patrolmen. Patrolmen like me were restricted to working the South Side, Burns Hill, and other black neighborhoods and haunts. Most black folks tended to think that all policemen were in it for the head-busting or the graft. And some had good reason to think that, especially if they'd been kicked around by those on the force with racist attitudes.

We had some good guys and some not-so-good guys. I tried to be one of the good guys, treating everyone with respect, but I have to admit, I didn't mind chasing criminals, black or white, and catching them. When you grow up in an unjust system like Jim Crow, you develop a very acute sense of what's right. Maybe that was why I was drawn to law enforcement, initially. Being a policeman made me feel more like part of a society that had marginalized me, and everyone who looked like me.

The job also gave me an outlet for the anger I'd repressed from all of those times someone called me a "nigger," or told me to use the back door, or to eat my food outside. One of the first things I'd heard when I joined the force was that black cops weren't supposed to arrest white people. I remember thinking, *To hell with that!*

ABOUT THREE WEEKS into the job, Graves and I received an emergency call that a white prisoner had escaped by beating up the cop who'd arrested him. The prisoner had taken off near Green Street in Burns Hill, not far from my grandparents' house.

I had a strong hunch about where the guy would go. There are not many places to hide on the Hill, but one of them had been my favorite place to play as a boy.

Boulding Branch Creek was little more than a drainage ditch that carried overflow from High Point Lake. My grandmother fretted over our playing along "the Branch," as everyone called it, because it was known to flash flood during heavy rains. She was afraid one of us might fall in and drown, but we loved it.

The banks were five feet high and hid us from adult eyes as we pretended to be exploring the Amazon. We used to play hide-and-seek for hours there, so when I heard there was an escaped prisoner in that area, I figured he'd try to use its high banks to cover his getaway.

Graves was driving the squad car, so I had him let me off at one end of the Branch and I told him to drive down to the other end and work his way back. Familiar fishy smells filled my nostrils as I climbed down the banks. No need to watch where I was going. My feet knew every stone and rut along the Branch.

I'd walked only about fifty yards when I saw the escaped prisoner huffing and humping along. He was coming fast, looking down at the rutted path alongside the creek so he didn't trip and fall into the water. He was nearly on top of me before he looked up into my gun.

"You can come on with me now, or I can drag you out of here," I said. "Either way, you are going back to jail."

But the man wasn't scared. He was indignant.

"You can't arrest me, nigger!"

Obviously my quarry had the mistaken impression that Jim Crow was part of the criminal code. I assured him that my arrest powers knew no boundaries of religion, class, or race.

"Like hell I can't arrest you," I said.

The runner responded by taking a roundhouse swing at my jaw. He missed, but my foot didn't. I kicked him square in the rear and sent him flying into the shining waters of the Branch. I then pulled him out and waved a blackjack in his face. The fight had gone out of him.

While I handcuffed my captive on the creek bank, my fellow officers poured in from all directions. Nobody suggested that I had violated any law, written or otherwise, in making my first arrest of a white man. When I escorted the former fugitive into the station house, the white desk sergeant had me sign the arrest warrant personally.

"He's a bad fella," the sergeant said. "You did a good job in bringing him in."

Over the next few days, word spread all over town that Officer Bob Brown had busted a white guy. Some thought it might cause me problems, but none came my way.

A few weeks later, I walked into one of the Washington Street barbershops where the local gossips and wise men were known to gather and discuss everybody's business. Upon seeing me, one of the old black guys in the shop said, "I hear you arrested that white man the other day."

I told him that I'd arrested a couple white men, actually.

"Well, you aren't supposed to be arresting white men," he said. "You're gonna stir things up."

I assured him that any man who broke the law on my turf was going to jail. I'd expected to take some flak for ignoring what had been a cultural norm, but this was one bit of Jim Crow that quietly faded away from High Point. Many doors remained closed, but a few were being pried open. For the town, and also for me.

AFTER A YEAR with the High Point Police Department, I was assigned to work with federal agents on a task force led by the Federal Bureau of Narcotics office in Greensboro. They were investigating drug dealers in the Greensboro, Winston-Salem, and High Point areas, and they needed some "fresh faces" to work undercover. Make that fresh *black* faces.

The focus was on drug dealing in black enclaves and neighborhoods. I was well known on Burns Hill and in the black churches around the state, but I'd never been one to frequent the region's seedier corners. They knew me in the choir lofts, but not in the darker dens. Still, as a young guy who also worked in law enforcement, I knew where the drug dealers and buyers hung out, or at least knew the right people to ask.

Jack Kelly, the FBN agent in charge of the Greensboro office, ran the investigation. I served as an undercover guide of sorts for the federal agents, donning my shabbiest clothes and working the bars, pool halls, back alleys, and street corners where deals went down. I went into it knowing there was plenty of weed on the street, but I was shocked to see the extent of hardcore drugs, especially opium. In the early 1950s, there had been a big increase in drug trafficking from Mexico into the United States. We discovered that crime organizations in New York City had been recruiting drug-carrying "mules" and dealers in the barrios and slums, to create a nationwide distribution network.

After about three months of investigation, we filed a report documenting what we'd found. Our initial reports triggered a six-month federal undercover operation led by Bill Jackson, a veteran federal narcotics investigator and the first black agent I'd met. He was smart, tough, and street-savvy, but he kept things laid-back because there were enough pressures on us on the street.

I looked up to him. When Bill Jackson suggested that I would make a good federal agent, it opened my eyes to greater possibilities. There were very few blacks, college-educated or otherwise, at that level of law enforcement. But when my special assignment to the FBN came to an end, Jack Kelly sent me application papers for a job at the bureau and offered to serve as my sponsor.

The job they offered was with the Federal Bureau of Narcotics' New York City division. Sallie was supportive. She loved the idea of exploring museums, seeing Broadway shows, and listening to live music in jazz clubs and concert halls. I had mixed feelings. Opportunities for a black male were limited, but it pained my heart to think about leaving High Point and my grandparents. After all, I'd left college out of concern for their health and welfare.

Practically speaking, the move made sense. Mama's and Daddy's health had stabilized, and we had other family members who could check in on them regularly. My increased earnings would allow me to help support them, too, whenever they needed extra money. But even as my application for the bureau job was under review, I couldn't bring myself to discuss the possibility of moving away from Mama. I kept putting off any mention of it, until one day Mama ambushed me when I stopped to see my grandparents after work.

"Sit down, Bobby, I've got something I want to ask you."

She was as serious as I'd ever seen her.

"Son, people all over town are talking about you," she said. "Everyone you've ever known seems to be getting phone calls and surprise visits from the FBI. Are you in serious trouble for some reason?"

Lord have mercy. I had no choice but to fess up.

"Mama, the FBI is doing a background check on me because I might be getting a job as a federal agent in New York City," I said.

She gave me the look I'd long dreaded. A sadness, and a look of resignation. Then she recovered.

"Why would you leave your good policeman job here?" she said.

I explained that the federal job was a big step up, a rare opportunity for a black man, and the kind of position that could open doors to even greater things one day. I assured her that if they offered the job to me and I took it, Sallie and I would return to visit on a regular basis, and I'd always be available if she needed me.

Mama listened and accepted it all. I could tell she was proud of me, but also torn. I couldn't quite hear the prayers she was sending up to ask God for strength, but I could certainly sense them.

"Bobby," she finally said, "I know you'll go up there and do a great job. Don't worry about us. Just remember to keep God in the middle of everything you do. As long as you surround yourself with God's armor, He will protect you and lift you up."

SALLIE AND I returned home from a brief vacation on June 3, 1958, and found a letter waiting from Harry Anslinger, the commissioner of the Federal Bureau of Narcotics. There was no warm welcome. The letter was more like a draft notice, saying I'd been appointed a federal agent.

I was ordered to report for duty two weeks later at the FBN's office in the federal building that takes up a whole block at 90 Church Street in Lower Manhattan.

It was the most impressive place I'd ever worked, for sure, and quite a move up from the High Point Police Department. I was twenty-three years old and it took me a while to adjust to big-city life, but Sallie loved the more sophisticated lifestyle. On our days off we hit all the museums, theaters, jazz clubs, and restaurants.

We had been naive about certain aspects of this move. I'd always thought of New York City as the epitome of an open and free society, a place where color didn't matter, and where opportunities were abundant. My naive delusions were dispelled after the first few days of apartment hunting on Manhattan's West Side.

There was no shortage of vacant apartments in our price range, but they weren't in our skin color range. I didn't see a single WHITES ONLY sign, but after several landlords refused to even show us their rental units, the message became abundantly clear.

"Robert, they don't want to rent to us here. They keep coming up with reasons and excuses, but it's because we're black. What can we do? Where can we live?"

New York City had fair-housing laws and no end of rules and regulations forbidding discriminatory practices by landlords. They meant diddly-squat. For the first three months, we had to stay at the Greystone Hotel near 91st Street and Broadway, cooking our dinners on a hot plate to save money, because we couldn't find a decent apartment anywhere except Harlem.

After hearing about our ordeal, one of my FBN coworkers, a black guy named Joe Daniels, eventually helped us find a place to live.

"There is more housing discrimination here than in most places in the South," he said. "My wife and I have a place in Brooklyn. Come out to visit us this weekend and we'll help you find something there."

With their assistance, we found a two-bedroom apartment at 1355 Union Street, in a Crown Heights brownstone off Eastern Parkway, just a few blocks from their place. We were able to swing the "high" rent of $100 a month, especially after Sallie found a job as a teletypist earning about $100 a week at a Mohawk Carpet distributor. She moved up quickly to the accounting department, and we settled in as a working couple in the city.

Needless to say, the area where I worked undercover was not featured on tourism brochures. The six black agents in our office rarely were assigned anywhere apart from Harlem and other areas that were mostly populated by minorities. We were sent to work undercover to make major drug buys and identify dealers and their sources, so we could move up the supply chain and bust those who were making the most off illegal drugs.

Often we had no backup, because few white agents could work in Harlem without being spotted as lawmen. The Mafia bosses ran most of the illicit drug trade. Many of their street lieutenants were Hispanic, and the low-level dealers were often African Americans. Black agents had the most dangerous jobs, but once our cases were made, the white supervisory agents would usually write the reports, claiming most of the credit.

That's not to say there weren't some white agents and supervisors who worked honorably. Many of them were good, hard-nosed, and fair men, but there were some real racist jerks too. Maybe they'd gotten away with it in the past, but those days were coming to an end, and I couldn't wait for the reckoning.

Chapter 4

FIGHTING THROUGH DARK TIMES

IN SEPTEMBER 1958, JUST A FEW MONTHS AFTER I JOINED the narcotics bureau, the Reverend Martin Luther King Jr. came to speak at the Convent Avenue Baptist Church in Harlem. He was there to promote his new book, *Stride Toward Freedom,* a memoir about the Montgomery bus boycott, which had established him as a national leader and put him on the cover of *Time* magazine.

King's book described the tactics his movement had used in Montgomery, and explained his belief in nonviolent protest and negotiation to bring about positive social change. Sallie and I were excited that our people were standing up against racism, and we were especially proud that Rosa Parks and Dr. King shared our church roots. But we were concerned, too.

Dr. King was stirring things up, which was admirable but also dangerous. The more prominent he became as a proponent of peaceful change, the bigger the target he became for those who hated him and his cause. During the Montgomery bus boycott, his home had been firebombed. Then, just a few days before the Harlem book signing, Dr. King was arrested and manhandled by police in Birmingham.

Still, Harlem seemed like the safest and most welcoming place for Dr. King in those days. The Convent Avenue Baptist Church offered a grand setting, with hand-carved altar rails and light fixtures that looked like antique gas lamps. Sallie and I were surprised that the church wasn't packed to the rafters, but the audience listened enthusiastically as Dr. King spoke about the successful Montgomery boycott and how he felt America needed to change. The budding "civil rights" movement, he promised, would change the country and the world for the better.

In those days, Dr. King had not yet developed the resonant speaking voice and staccato cadence that would eventually transfix and inspire audiences around the world. Like me, he was still in his twenties, and he still seemed to be growing into his leadership role. Sallie thought his message was good, but after listening to this man who would become one of the world's most famous orators, she confessed that he nearly put her to sleep that night. Sallie could be a tough judge.

After his speech, we stood in line to shake the hand of Dr. King and introduce ourselves. I was surprised at how soft his hands seemed. Sallie thought he was interesting, but not particularly charismatic. "I thought he seemed like a nice young man," she offered on the way home, "but he wasn't as dynamic as I thought he'd be, and you are much better-looking, Robert!"

Years later, when we became close friends, I told Martin about Sallie's initial assessment of him, and we had a good laugh over it. For the sake of diplomacy, I may have left out the part about me being more handsome, though.

Despite Sallie's assessment, I was impressed with Dr. King that night. His vision for equality was inspiring, and his humility impressed me. He seemed more laid-back than I'd expected from an activist, not at all aggressive or self-promoting. He had the sincerity of someone who was truly dedicated to a cause.

BUT IT TURNS OUT I had been right to fear for Dr. King's safety. The following Saturday, September 20, I was working a Harlem case with another agent, Roland Copeland, when our police radio monitor sent us on another mission.

The report said King had been attacked and stabbed during a book signing at Blumstein's department store, next to the Hotel Theresa in Harlem. My first thought was, *What white person is crazy enough to come into Harlem and attack a black leader of Dr. King's standing?*

We were already patrolling in the area, so we drove to Harlem Hospital, where Dr. King had been taken in an ambulance. I'd never seen so many police cars in that neighborhood. I'm sure they feared a riot would be set off. That didn't happen because, as we soon learned, the attacker had been a mentally disturbed black woman. She was a paranoid schizophrenic who'd ranted and cursed him for being a communist after the attack. She hadn't even bothered to run after stabbing Dr. King.

The attack very nearly killed him. Surgeons had to remove two ribs and some of his breastbone to get out the seven-inch knife. The X-rays showed that the tip of the blade had lodged between his heart and lung, and stopped just short of puncturing his main artery. The next day, the *New York Times* reported that if King had so much as sneezed, he likely would have died. In his speeches, he'd often say that he'd been just a sneeze away from death.

The assault deeply concerned me, and many others who had come to see Martin as a young leader of great promise. It seemed like whenever one of our people made a step toward prominence, something terrible happened. The fact that he survived, and declared his intention to continue on his mission, was inspiring. I kept close watch on Dr. King after that in the media, hoping our paths would cross again.

SEVEN MONTHS LATER, I encountered another major figure of those times. Our meeting also went down as the only time I can remember being adequately protected while working undercover as a federal narcotics agent.

The heavy security backup was due to the presence of Robert F. Kennedy, the future U.S. attorney general. In those days, Bobby Kennedy was the chief counsel for the Senate Labor Rackets Committee, and he'd shown up in New York to observe a drug deal I'd set up as part of an investigation into organized crime's drug operations.

For six months or so, I'd been working a bunch of cases, setting up street buys, when my group leader called me into his office the morning of April 20, 1959. He wanted to know if I planned on making any buys within the next day or two. I had a couple of dealers who were ripe. I told him something could probably be arranged.

"We're interested in anything you can do right away," he said. "The Senate Rackets Committee's top lawyer is looking into the mob's drug operations. He's asked to shadow one of our agents to witness him making a heroin buy from a dealer linked to the mob. You're his man."

And so, the next night, I gave the brother of the future president of the United States a real-life demonstration worthy of a Broadway show. In fact, I did meet a dealer on Broadway, a hundred blocks north of the theaters, at the edge of Harlem. There, I bought two ounces of heroin while Bobby Kennedy watched with his guards in a car parked at the end of the block.

I didn't arrest the dealer after the transaction. It was his lucky day. Instead, after making the buy, I took Bobby Kennedy and his men to my downtown office for a lengthy conversation about the flow of narcotics on the streets, the mob's involvement in drug sales, the level of violence in the drug trade, and the impact that illicit drugs had on people in Harlem and other neighborhoods.

Kennedy hardly looked old enough to buy a beer in a tavern, but he was focused and intense in his questioning. He wanted to know how the mob's distribution networks worked, what the markup was on the street, and who oversaw the street dealers.

Bobby was respectful toward me, and seemed appreciative of the work I was doing and the dangers that accompanied undercover operations. He didn't treat me like a lowly street agent. He treated me as a professional. I liked that he wasn't arrogant, even though he had come from wealth and had an Ivy League education. He seemed intent on understanding the problems and addressing them. It brought to mind something my grandmother had told me: "You can only be a leader if people want to follow you."

I came away feeling Bobby Kennedy was a man of substance with a promising future, which is why I wrote him a letter a few days later. I offered to help him in any way he needed, noting that I had many contacts among Negro leaders in the South. I didn't say it in my letter to Kennedy, but later I told my bosses with the bureau that given the number of bodyguards he commanded that night, I'd go undercover with him anytime.

ABOUT A YEAR after I joined the bureau, my superiors recruited a dynamic young Bedford-Stuyvesant native named Earl G. Graves, who'd been honorably discharged from the Airborne Rangers Special Forces Group. Earl was a graduate of Morgan State University, a former Green Beret, and not inclined to take a back seat on anybody's bus.

Growing up in the South, I'd never met another black man quite like Earl. He was as brash, bold, and assertive as the Manhattan skyline. He sometimes wore his green beret to work, but otherwise he dressed in fitted suits with extra room in the shoulders. That's where he kept the holsters for his Wild West sidearms—two pearl-handled .38-caliber pistols, as I recall.

Earl was fascinated with the frontier exploits of the Buffalo Soldiers, and he had that sort of mythic presence himself. He was a big, strapping guy, six-two, and fighting-fit from his military training. Even then, he wore his sideburns extra-long, though not as long as the muttonchops that would become his trademark one day.

Earl's tenure with the FBN was brief. He'd been one of the first African Americans to reach the rank of captain in the Airborne Rangers, so Earl was very good at giving orders, not so interested in taking them. Especially if they were coming from racist supervisors.

Shortly after joining the bureau, Earl came up to me and said he'd had enough. "I'm not going to let these white guys use me to make their cases so they can take all the credit," he vented.

Earl had a powerful entrepreneurial drive, mighty ambitions, and zero desire to blend in with lowlifes as an undercover agent. He quit and soon began a legendary career as publisher of *Black Enterprise* magazine. Earl was a tireless champion of black business development. He was active in the Democratic Party and always a good friend and confidant, even when our political paths diverged.

I had a higher tolerance, and maybe fewer options, than Earl did back then. There were some early signs, however, that made me wonder if this was a career path I wanted to continue following. Racism was entrenched within the bureau, and there were other strange things that bothered me about my supervisors. They seemed to want to isolate me from my fellow agents, both black and white.

When I first joined the bureau, my supervisor said it would be a good idea for me to not "socialize," or even fraternize in the office, with the other agents. He said they wanted to limit my contacts to protect my identity for undercover work. But I found it unsettling that I wasn't supposed to trust even my fellow agents.

I also knew for a fact that I'd been put under surveillance in my first few weeks on the job, as if they didn't trust me. They usually sent me out with wads of cash, thousands of dollars, to make major drug buys in Harlem and other danger spots. Two other agents accompanied me to serve as backup, although I often suspected they weren't all that interested in protecting me.

After a couple of years with the FBN, I'd begun to think about changing careers to something safer, maybe even trying to find a way to run my own business. I'd seen a television documentary on a famous public relations man, and it mentioned a book called *Effective Public Relations* by Scott M. Cutlip and Allen H. Center, who were pioneers in the field.

I read the book and found it fascinating. They described public relations as a service business that provided entrée into all sorts of opportunities. There were many facets to it, but the job mostly involved helping clients craft and protect a good public image that drew customers to them and their brands. The other major role of public relations firms that really interested me was troubleshooting for clients who had problems or potential problems that might tarnish the image of their company or brand, and hurt business. The term "crisis management" wasn't used much back in those days, but that's what they call that service today.

I was intrigued by the strategies laid out in the book. I'd always had a natural ability for solving problems and persuading people. I also liked that public relations seemed like a business you could start without having to invest huge sums in training, equipment, or real estate. In my Boy Scout troop back in High Point, I was usually the one chosen by my fellow scouts to represent them in the mock trials we held if someone had broken the rules. Our scout leader, the Reverend Warren Steele, always said I had a future as a trial lawyer.

I'd enjoyed the social life in the city, but working with addicts, drug dealers, prostitutes, murderers, and thieves was taking a toll. I yearned to get out of the city and back into the piney woods and warmer sun of my native state.

Without telling Sallie, who had grown to love city life over the last two years, I put out feelers to folks back in High Point. There were several things calling me home. My grandparents were at the top of the list, but I also felt my hometown needed me.

North Carolina, and particularly the area where I grew up, had become a focal point of civil rights demonstrations. The first major protests began on February 1, 1960, when four freshmen at my former school, North Carolina Agricultural and Technical State College, staged what they initially called a "sit-down" demonstration at the whites-only lunch counter of the Woolworth's store in downtown Greensboro.

Their protests went on for five months. More than five hundred blacks and whites participated. Later known as "sit-ins," the demonstrations triggered a series of similar events across the country. I was inspired by the defiant pride of the black demonstrators and their supporters, even though I was unnerved by the jeers and threats they received from contemptuous whites. I saw the potential for violence in their increasingly heated clashes.

The most frequent target of those early civil rights demonstrations was Woolworth's, the Walmart of that era. The national retail chain had thousands of stores around the country, and while Woolworth's wasn't the only segregated lunch counter in Greensboro, local blacks found it particularly galling that the Woolworth's chain enforced segregated seating only in the South. In Northern states, blacks and whites ate side by side at Woolworth's and most other variety stores and restaurants.

By the start of the second week of the Greensboro sit-in, similar demonstrations arose all over the area. Raleigh, Durham, and Winston-Salem each had protests, as did my hometown, which really concerned me.

Mary Lou Andrews, a fifteen-year-old student at William Penn High School who would go on to a long life in community service, organized the protest at the High Point Woolworth's. She recruited about twenty-five other teens to join her, and several adult civil rights activists. They were joined by the Reverend Fred Shuttlesworth, a cofounder of the Southern Christian Leadership Conference, who just happened to be in town.

Days into the protest, a group of whites pelted the black kids with snowballs that had been packed with broken glass. The protestors responded by throwing snowballs and other things. There were some minor injuries. Police broke up the fight.

The situation grew worse over the next few days. Riots erupted between blacks and whites in downtown High Point. More than eighty police officers were brought in to control the crowds and make arrests. The mayor of High Point formed an interracial human relations committee, one of the first of its kind during this era, to resolve issues related to racial tension. The group recommended the integration of lunch counters, but it would take a couple of years for that to happen.

Most of the small town's business owners realized that integration was inevitable, and even desirable from a business standpoint. Often, they had no problem opening up to black customers. Their main concern in many cases was alienating white customers who still held on to racist beliefs or fears. There were die-hard racists in High Point, certainly, but there were also many older residents who simply were threatened by any change in the social order.

Friends from High Point were calling me in New York and asking for my advice. My hometown needed me. It was frustrating to be so far away and unable to help. The spread of these protests convinced me that the movement was going to escalate. I wanted to be a part of leading change for the better. I began searching for ways to get back home. I called the offices of two politicians whose campaigns I'd worked for, and asked their aides if they had any opportunities for a public relations man on their teams.

When I didn't drum up any job prospects, I decided to make my own. I told my supervisor, George Gaffney, that I was leaving the FBN to go back to High Point and start a public relations business. He bluntly told me I was making a mistake.

"Your people can't even eat in a restaurant back in North Carolina. If you are going to do something with your life, you should stay with the bureau in the city," he said. "You're a damn fool if you quit and go back home. You could retire from the bureau in twenty years and then open up your own office here in Manhattan."

Damn fool or not, I didn't see much future in the life of an undercover drug agent working all hours of the day and night in the most violent corners of several large cities. I didn't mind taking risks—as long as I could share in the rewards. That wasn't going to happen in the FBN as it was then structured. Most of the white supervisors never seemed to give a damn about black agents, their families, their goals, or their safety.

In fact, my decision to leave the bureau was initially blocked by a bullying supervisor who assigned me to "the Valachi watch," a particularly dangerous assignment. Joe Valachi was a career criminal and low-level Mafia gofer who had worked his way up in the organization as a hit man, enforcer, numbers operator, and drug pusher. After years of trailing him, the FBN had finally nailed him on drug charges in 1959. We had him under heavy guard while awaiting sentencing, because the mob wanted him dead. They were afraid he'd try to cut a deal to reduce his sentence by giving us information about the crime syndicate he'd worked for.

I saw this last-minute assignment as a trap that could keep me in the bureau for many more months, or get me shot by mob assassins gunning for Valachi. My bosses demanded that I keep working at the bureau until Valachi was locked up, which could take several months. I reminded them of the Emancipation Proclamation that freed me from slavery.

When that didn't work, I called in a favor from a friend, Bill Cochrane, who was an assistant to U.S. senator B. Everett Jordan of North Carolina, whom I'd campaigned for back home.

"Bill, I've turned in my resignation with the bureau here, but my immediate supervisor is refusing to let me quit," I said. "Instead, he's assigned me to be Valachi's bodyguard until they can get him locked away."

"Don't worry about a thing," my friend told me. "Go home and pack."

The senator's staffer made some calls, and my bosses were ordered to let me resign as planned.

And so, after two and a half years, I said goodbye to New York City and my life of undercover crime. I felt lucky to get out unscathed and alive. Sallie had taken some convincing about this big move, but as always, she supported me. We would miss our friends and all of the attractions of big-city life, but I would not miss working for supervisors who saw me as dispensable and dependent. I had come to know many well-educated, ambitious, and defiant blacks in New York. They were starting their own businesses and taking charge of their own destinies. I wanted to take charge of mine.

For generations, most black men and women had thought factory work or "a government job" was their best and only career option for financial security. We owed those generations our gratitude for the sacrifices they made, but we were eager to build upon their efforts and move beyond being employed to being employers. Instead of living paycheck to paycheck, we wanted to build wealth, and be leaders in business and our communities.

My destination was a small office on Washington Street in High Point, the same street where I'd shined shoes as a boy. This time, I was setting up shop for my own business as Robert J. Brown, public relations man.

PART TWO

Chapter 5

QUIET VICTORIES

S TARTING A BUSINESS IS NEVER EASY, AND IT'S EVEN HARDER when you also have a bunch of street-corner skeptics mocking you every day on your way in to the office.

Most folks in High Point made it clear that they thought I was crazy for quitting my federal job in New York City. My biggest chorus of local critics were the old guys swigging from brown paper bags along Washington Street.

The old drunks would laugh and take potshots at me when they weren't pulling on their bottles: "Brown ain't gonna do nothin' with that business." More than a few suggested that I'd probably be back shining shoes and busting rags in a short time.

I used those taunts as motivation. Lord knows, I needed all the motivation I could get. I opened my public relations firm in High Point in January of 1961. My first office was a rented space above the Ritz Theater on Washington Street. Despite the name on the building, I wasn't exactly putting on the ritz. The theater had been our town's only movie house for blacks, but the former hot spot had fallen on hard times and shut down.

My one-room office was furnished with one desk, a chair for Sallie (who was working as my secretary), and one for me. On the desk sat the telephone and a skimpy Rolodex with maybe two or three names on its cards.

The sign on the door said B&C ASSOCIATES. The "C" represented my old friend Albert Campbell. He'd been my business partner for the first few weeks, but Albert left after he realized, quite correctly, that we were in for a painfully slow start-up phase. To this day, the name of my business remains B&C Associates, despite Albert's departure to the local fire department, where he became the town's first black firefighter.

I was committed to making this plan work, so I spent many long hours making cold calls to drum up business. I must've dialed my way through the Yellow Pages of every town within 100 miles—High Point, Greensboro, Winston-Salem. I also worked the streets, using whatever connections I had. It was a struggle.

A few weeks after setting up shop, I ran into our local state representative, Joe Hunt, whom I'd campaigned for when I was a local policeman. At first, we just talked about the old days. Then I told him about my new business and probably overshared, confessing that things were so bad, I had fallen behind on the payments for my 1960 Rambler. (I didn't tell him that I'd taken to hiding it behind the Carolina Pool Room so the repo man couldn't find it.)

Joe was a self-made man. He knew how difficult it could be to start a business, so he pulled out his wallet and handed me a $100 bill.

"This is a retainer," he said. "Put me on your client list."

It was a jolt of good fortune, but Joe didn't stop there. A few days later, he sent another client to me—one that helped set me up for a long career of resolving disputes, building bridges, and working for positive social change.

The client's name was Mose Kiser, and he ran Guilford Dairy, a farmers' cooperative that delivered milk in the area. Along with the milk business, the co-op owned a dozen or so ice cream shops around Greensboro, Durham, Burlington, and High Point—shops that had long followed local Jim Crow laws, refusing to allow black customers to sit and eat their treats at the snack bar. The dairy bar discrimination had gone on for as long as anyone could remember, but a few months before I moved back to High Point, local black leaders had threatened to boycott the dairy bars if they didn't let blacks sit inside. They also wanted Kiser to start hiring blacks as delivery truck drivers, which was only fair since so many of the co-op's customers were black folks.

For me, it was good timing. I'd read that the key to public relations was to offer yourself to clients as a problem solver, so I had decided that crisis management and mediation would be one of my public relations specialties. With the civil rights movement picking up steam, there was no shortage of crises for local businesses who'd been targeted by demonstrators, so I targeted those same businesses as clients, figuring I could get them to see that shutting out blacks wasn't just discriminatory, it was also bad business. Given the right incentives, I believed most owners would do the right thing.

When I met him, I could tell that Mose Kiser was not racist. But he had to answer to the co-op members, all of whom had to live in a community where many whites still favored segregation. Mose didn't know where to begin in handling the black protestors, many of whom he had known for decades.

"Bob, can you help me figure out how to make things right for the colored folks without driving away my white customers?" he asked. "I'm caught between a rock and a hard place here."

I told him that I had some thoughts on how to resolve his problem without causing a lot of grief. We shook hands, and Mose asked his assistant general manager, Max Hovis, to negotiate a fee with me. I really had no idea what to charge, but I desperately needed some cash flow. Sallie and I had moved in with her mother to save rent. I barely had enough to help with the groceries or pay for my office. "Max, if you'll pay me $250 a month plus expenses, I can give you advice and help whenever you need it," I proposed.

When he agreed to sign a one-year contract, I wanted to dance in the street. Then I went straight to work. I spoke with the dairy co-op's managers and employees, including the few blacks who worked in low-level positions. Next, I met with Dr. George Simkins

Jr., the president of the NAACP in Greensboro. George had found success both as a dentist and as an activist in the community. Years earlier, he and some friends had tried to integrate the segregated city golf course, getting arrested after their round. They eventually won the court fight, and when the desegregated course reopened, Dr. Simkins was the first golfer to tee off.

I told George that my goal was to convince the dairy co-op members that discriminating against black customers was hurting their business. But when I took that message to the white co-op members, their main concern was that white customers might stop coming in if blacks were allowed to sit down. My response to them—and to the many clients who followed—was that the push for racial equality was an undeniable force. I reminded them that blacks represented at least a third of the co-op's customers. If they boycotted the dairy bars and milk delivery businesses, the co-op would take a huge hit.

"Change is coming," I said, "and how you handle it now will impact your business for years to come. The businesses that don't recognize the growing power of black consumers will not survive."

My approach was not confrontational. I just provided them with information and a long-term perspective. The co-op members were cautious, but they eventually agreed to desegregate, gradually and without fanfare. We were all surprised at how quickly white customers accepted it. Soon, business was booming.

Quiet victories are the best, to my way of thinking, and this was one in which every party benefited. The dairy expanded its customer base, and the black community won fair treatment and increased opportunities. In the process, I developed a client relationship that lasted many years. Before long, it would serve as a launchpad for even bigger things.

————

THE PEACEFUL RESOLUTION of that crisis set a pattern for my career as a public relations man, though I had a long road to travel before becoming financially secure. I enjoyed the process of bringing both sides together. I felt like I was making a difference in the community.

The only problem was that I needed to make more money than my High Point and Greensboro clients could afford to pay me. For more than a year I worked small local accounts, struggling to stay ahead of the bill collectors. As much as I loved my hometown, there was not a lot of walk-in business there.

Finally, in the spring of 1961, I decided to gas up my Rambler and travel the East Coast in search of corporate clients. I'd researched companies that were dealing with race, labor, and community relations problems, and I created a customized pitch for each one. I also targeted the big advertising and public relations agencies like McCann Erickson and Carl Byoir in New York City.

For about two weeks, I worked my way up the coast, stopping at corporate headquarters and agencies along the way. By the time I reached New York, I hadn't landed a single client. I didn't have enough money to get a hotel room, so I slept in the trusty Rambler, which had a front seat that folded back that I could use as a bed.

I was twenty-six years old and confident that I could take care of myself, so I parked my car in gas station parking lots, or on 10th Avenue under the West Side Highway. The neighborhood wasn't exactly safe, but I had my .357 Magnum and the switchblade I had carried during my days in law enforcement.

Patrol officers would check on me from time to time, and I told them I was just grabbing some rest before heading back to North Carolina. I showered at the 34th Street YMCA for a fifty-cent charge, then hit the street in my business suit and well-polished shoes. You'd never know that I hadn't spent the night in a suite at the Waldorf Astoria. (Or so I hoped.)

My first stop in town was the Woolworth Building at 233 Broadway. I thought I could help the national retail chain in the same way that I'd helped the dairy co-op back home. Representing such a huge corporation would be more work, of course, but I was betting that the paychecks would be more substantial as well.

I boldly marched up to the reception area.

"My name is Robert J. Brown, and I would like to speak with the chairman of the board about a business proposition," I said.

I was wearing a silk repp tie and the most expensive shirt and suit I owned, both of which I'd bought on the installment plan. I felt confident in my presentation, but when I made my request, the receptionist gave me a look that made me feel like I'd stumbled in wearing dirty bib overalls and carrying a potato hoe.

"He is unavailable at this time," she said, before taking an intense interest in her fingernails.

"Well then, I'll just wait until he is available," I said. "I'm sure he will be interested in my proposition."

She gave me another appraisal and decided to try another tactic.

"Maybe you should speak with our vice president of public relations, Mr. E. F. Harrigan," she said.

"If he is available, that would be a good start," I said.

"I will see if he has a few minutes to spare," she said, coolly. "Can you please take a seat in the waiting area?"

I had the distinct impression that she was passing me on to someone trained to handle uninvited visitors. Woolworth's variety stores were under the gun from civil rights activists, and I'm sure this guardian of the gate was rattled by the sudden appearance of a black man at the door.

I'd been brushed off in this manner all up and down the East Coast, so when the PR man appeared, I could tell he wanted to get rid of me quickly. He was a straitlaced, buttoned-down guy in a dark suit. Cordial and businesslike, he had the air of a dedicated corporate soldier.

Mr. Harrigan likely thought I was from a local church group or the NAACP, looking for a charitable donation of some kind. I'd run into that mentality often on these cold calls. Corporate America had yet to accept blacks as a legitimate presence in the higher echelons of the business world.

But I set him straight right away.

"Mr. Harrigan, I am a public relations executive and I have had considerable experience in the Southern United States helping business clients develop better relations with the black community, including those in the civil rights movement," I said. "I would like to work with your company and serve as a bridge to help F. W. Woolworth resolve any conflicts and build its business with Negro consumers in the South and across the country."

He listened and, to my surprise, seemed intrigued.

"Mr. Brown, I only have a few minutes to spare, but come into my office and tell me a little more about what you might be able to do for us," he said.

We talked there for more than an hour about my background in law enforcement and my success with Guilford Dairy. I outlined my strategy for helping Woolworth's in the same way. He listened with interest, but then told me that Woolworth's had already hired the largest public relations firm in the world, Carl Byoir & Associates, to help with its "Negro problems."

I held out hope, because he added that Byoir might be interested in working with me as a consultant, given my contacts and knowledge of the issues. He then called Bob Wood, a vice president at Byoir, and told him that he was sending someone over "who might prove helpful with Woolworth's challenges."

After hanging up, Mr. Harrigan said that Mr. Wood had agreed to give me a few minutes if I could get to Byoir's office at 10 East 42nd Street in the next hour. Again, I wasn't sure if this was a handoff or a brush-off, but I certainly couldn't pass up the chance to make a connection with a powerhouse PR firm. Carl Byoir &

Associates was a dominant force in the corporate world, with a client list that included major brands such as A&P grocery stores, Eastern Railroad, Johnson Wax, and Kimberly-Clark.

I left the Woolworth Building and hustled to Byoir's headquarters several blocks away. Bob Wood met me in a reception area. A white guy of medium build, he wore suspenders and a look of caution, but within our first few minutes of conversation, I could tell he was intrigued with my pitch. My allotted fifteen minutes extended to three hours.

Bob Wood knew his business, but he'd never been ordered to enter a restaurant through a back door or sit in the back of a bus. Public relations was a white man's game back then. Most whites in corporate America had very little contact with blacks, and they didn't understand that the world we lived in was much different from theirs.

"I believe my experiences in resolving racial issues and building bridges can add a unique service to your firm," I said.

To my lasting gratitude, Mr. Wood recognized just that in our first meeting.

"Mr. Brown, you have made some very good points," he said. "Your timing just might be very good. We have been wrestling with how to help our clients with these concerns."

I think he was intrigued to meet a black man who offered himself as a bridge between his corporate clients and increasingly agitated black activists who were fed up with discrimination.

At the end of our meeting, we shook hands.

"We will be working together," Mr. Wood said.

I thought our discussion had gone extremely well, yet I still worried that I was being played. *Maybe he was just picking my brain so he could steal my strategies,* I thought. *Maybe he's just really good at handling unwanted walk-ins.*

Years later, Bob Wood admitted to me that while he had believed I could be a valuable resource for his company, he'd doubted the firm's management team would want to hire me. They were conservative white guys too. Bringing me on to advise them might seem like an admission that they couldn't handle this challenge on their own.

I returned to High Point exhausted, without any more clients signed up. My spirits were sagging. Maybe the brown-paper-bag boys on the street corner were right. Maybe I should have stuck to my government job.

The next day, I went to see my grandmother. She asked me to take her to visit a friend in Winston-Salem. I had to tell her that I didn't have enough money for gas, even at twenty cents a gallon. She pulled a handkerchief out of her blouse and produced a $20 bill.

On the way to see her friend, she consoled me. "If you have enough courage and faith, and you are willing to sacrifice and work hard, nothing can stop you, son," she said.

She'd told me the same thing many, many times as I was growing up. She may have whispered it to Bill and me as we slept. But the stakes seemed so much higher now. I'd never felt so burdened with pressure. I prayed all the way to Winston-Salem and all the way home, too.

When my office phone rang early in the morning a few days later, my first thought was to let it keep ringing because it was probably the bank wanting the keys to my car. Instead, it was the key to my future.

"Mr. Brown, we would like to offer you a consulting contract to help us with Woolworth's and maybe some other clients as well," Bob Wood said.

"Thank you so much, sir. You won't regret your decision," I said.

I'm sure my voice cracked. I could barely hold back the tears of relief.

My good sense failed me momentarily, and I told Mr. Wood that he was a credit to his race. I'm sure he found the remark strange, but he let it slide.

"Can you catch a plane to New York today? We'd like to start working on strategies," he said.

I had other commitments that day, but I promised to be in his office the following morning. I had to borrow the plane fare for that trip. But over the next six months, I made $80,000 in fees as a consultant to Byoir. That was more money than my total life earnings up to that point.

This bounty was especially sweet, because most of it came from the F. W. Woolworth Company, the same retailer that had forbidden me to sit at their lunch counters or drink at their whites-only water fountain. Over the next three decades, I would make millions in my work for Woolworth's, and become close friends with many of their top people. But every time I cashed one of their checks, I thought back to those days when I was turned away from their lunch counters, and I'd think: *Nope, it's not enough. You still owe me!*

The unforgettable sting of racism drove me throughout my lifetime to prove myself and to make a difference in this world. I had anger, but I controlled it and directed it to a higher purpose, just as my grandmother had taught me.

SHORTLY AFTER taking on Woolworth's as my first big client, I set out on a national tour of stores in the communities where demonstrators were most active. My goal was not to pacify either side, but to bring them together and work out a solution that benefited both the client and their customers. I assured clients that ending discrimination was the best long-range business strategy, because the black consumer market was growing and expanding. My stance with the protestors was that I shared their goals, and if they were patient and trusted me, I could help them bring change as their man inside the white establishment.

Working for Byoir and its clients, I traveled the country assessing and mediating civil rights protests against Woolworth's and other businesses. Most were in the South, but my work also took me to Detroit, Chicago, Washington, DC, Los Angeles, Portland, and many other locations.

In each community where civil rights protests or boycotts were taking place, I'd meet with the targeted businesses' employees and managers to learn their points of view. Then I would seek out the local civil rights and student leaders to hear what they had to say. My strategy for mediating these conflicts was usually to work with local ministers to try to set up community relations councils, also known as human rights or "good neighbor" councils. The bottom line in every case was to make sure everyone involved benefited in some way.

In each town, I tried to meet with Woolworth's managers and employees, and also with the local protest leaders. I often had something of an "in" with the protestors, thanks to my days of tagging along with Mama on her regular gospel tours of AME Zion churches.

There is a long history of civil rights activism in the African Methodist Episcopal Zion Church. In the 1800s, many AME Zion churches in the North and South served as way stations in the Underground Railroad. Pioneering freedom fighters such as Harriet Tubman, Frederick Douglass, and Sojourner Truth had been members. So were many of the local activists behind the Woolworth's demonstrations.

I sought out the ministers for AME Zion and other black churches. If I did not know the local ministers personally, we often had friends in common from my regular trips to church conferences and conventions as a boy. These church connections proved invaluable. It also helped that my uncle, the Reverend Arthur

Marshall, was a prominent AME Zion minister and civil rights fighter who later became a bishop in the AME Zion church.

Back then, blacks didn't have access to most of the social and business networks that whites built. We weren't invited or welcome to join, in most cases. Surely the white business network was a much wider and far more powerful force. Theirs was based on contacts made in elite prep schools, colleges, fraternal groups, country clubs, civic organizations, charities, and their own churches.

But my network had its own strengths. Our ties were formed in shared suffering, and they were strengthened by a solidarity and determination forged over years of exclusion, discrimination, oppression, and victimization by the white majority. We may have belonged to different churches or differed philosophically on many issues. But the majority of blacks had one common, overriding goal in those days: bringing Jim Crow to its knees.

That's not to say that I had it easy when trying to bring protestors and corporate leaders together. The very mention of my first big client brought curses and raised fists among black activists. These were tense times, and it was commonly understood that even a "brother" was not always a true brother. There were times when I'd encounter outright hostility from protestors and their leaders. Some wanted to write me off as a sellout, or an Uncle Tom. I had to earn their respect before I could bridge the gap, which was often a difficult thing to do.

In the early summer of 1961, I believe, I went to Norfolk, Virginia, where black college students had been leading protests and demonstrations at the local Woolworth's store. Upon arrival, I learned that local black leaders were meeting at a church to discuss strategy. Somebody invited me to the meeting, but when I walked in, one of the guys jumped up and said, "This is a closed meeting, we don't want any Uncle Tom Negroes in here. We are trying to do some black-folk business."

This was bad news. If I wanted to build bridges and fight for racial equality, I could not be seen as a mere mouthpiece or shill for the white establishment.

I said a silent prayer to control my anger. *Lord, help them see that I am on their side, fighting for their cause because it is my cause, too.* I understood why they were suspicious. They didn't know me, and I had showed up in a suit, saying I represented a corporation that had taken their money while denying their humanity and worth.

The guy who had invited me was embarrassed at the catcalls. He stood up and started to introduce me, but I interrupted him.

"Let me speak for myself," I said. "I was born and raised in the South, and I've been through as much as any man in this room. My grandma's daddy was a slave bought and sold in North Carolina. I've been rebuked and scorned by white people, and I know as much as anyone in this room about segregation, being held down and shut out from opportunities. I'm here to be helpful, and if you want my help then I'll help; if not, I'll be gone. I'm not going to take any grief from anybody, black or white."

Straight talk has always worked best for me in situations like this. And sure enough, my sincerity came through. Even the guy who'd threatened to throw me out later had dinner with me. We became friends and visited each other many times over the years. I had similar experiences throughout my travels. Generally, all I had to do was talk a bit about my hometown and my church background to establish common ground, make connections, and build trust.

"I've dealt with racism all my life," I would say. "So I share your cause, and I consider you heroes for taking a stand. I'm here to help you and my client find a peaceful resolution that results not just in ending discrimination, but in opening up jobs and opportunities for you that benefit everyone in the black community. I want to support your efforts and serve as a resource. If you need a bus to take you to a demonstration, I can arrange to pay for it. If you need meals while you are on the road, or to pay for a room, just let me know."

Sometimes I paid out of my own pocket to get it done. More often, I used money made available by my clients to establish goodwill. Initially, I worked with Woolworth's top public relations man, E. F. Harrigan, as my primary contact with the corporate leadership. Once I earned his trust, his bosses began inviting me to roundtable meetings in the company's executive dining room, where I spoke with top executives and board members about civil rights issues around the country.

These were white executives who had very little contact with black America. I cleared up misconceptions and false impressions, introducing them to a consumer market that they'd never fully understood. I won their complete trust, and F. W. Woolworth Company would go on to desegregate their last store in early 1964, as I recall. But I kept working with them for more than three decades. They gave me the freedom, and the money, to create programs, initiatives, and outreach to the black community. I recruited blacks to serve as managers, corporate executives, and members of their board of directors during that period.

I also convinced the F. W. Woolworth Company to stock products for black consumers made by black-owned companies, like Johnson Products in Chicago. The founder, George E. Johnson, was the son of a sharecropper and a friend of mine. He'd never been able to get the big chain stores to carry his popular lines of Ultra Sheen and Afro Sheen hair-care products. But getting into Woolworth's stores opened the doors to other chains, and his business grew into a multimillion-dollar enterprise that, in 1971, became the first black-owned company listed on the American Stock Exchange.

I can't say it was easy, standing between protestors and the businesses that had shut them out. But from the very beginning, my mission was always guided by my grandmother's voice: *Bobby, you can never do wrong by doing what's right.*

Chapter 6

THE STRENGTH TO SERVE

O NCE I LANDED THE F. W. WOOLWORTH COMPANY AS A CLIent, I became a very busy man. Much of my work was done in Atlanta, home base to the top civil rights leaders and strategists. Those were hectic, exhilarating times, especially once my work on behalf of my corporate clients led me to the doorstep of Dr. Martin Luther King Jr.

In March 1960, just a month after the Woolworth's demonstrations in downtown Greensboro, the action moved to Atlanta and from there spread quickly across the country. Students from Atlanta's six black colleges organized their own series of sit-ins to protest segregated lunch counters, targeting Woolworth's variety stores and also Rich's Department Store, another major Atlanta retailer. During those protests, more than fifty demonstrators were arrested, including Dr. King and his brother, A. D. King.

Dr. King had moved back to Atlanta in 1960 after six years in Montgomery, Alabama. He joined his father as co-pastor of Atlanta's Ebenezer Baptist Church in 1960, but his primary reason for returning was to live closer to the headquarters of the Southern Christian Leadership Conference, which he had cofounded with a group of activist ministers in January of 1957. The new civil rights organization was dedicated to fostering nonviolent social change by mobilizing protestors and demonstrators against discrimination and segregation. The SCLC also backed leadership training, education, and voter registration drives for blacks.

The formation of the SCLC was a call to action that I could not resist. I made a special effort to get to know the organization's leaders whenever I was in Atlanta. Business had little to do with it, to be honest. I believed their cause was vitally important, and wanted to help them in any way possible.

I put out the word of my interest in the SCLC's activities through my growing list of contacts in Atlanta's business and church communities. One of those contacts, Stanley Scott, would become a lifelong friend. He was then a young reporter for the *Atlanta Daily World,* founded by his uncle.

Stanley and I hit it off immediately, and he introduced me to many other movers and shakers in Atlanta's black community. I was having lunch with him one day in an Auburn Avenue restaurant just a block from his newspaper office when Stanley looked up, spotted a friend, and said to me: "Bob, this is someone I want you to meet, he could use your help."

Stanley led me across the restaurant to the table of the Reverend Wyatt Tee Walker, the first full-time executive head of the Southern Christian Leadership Conference. Wyatt didn't say much as I explained my work on behalf of Woolworth's and other clients. He seemed skeptical about my business connections to the white establishment.

He warmed up quickly after I mentioned that I'd attended his alma mater, Virginia Union, about five years after he graduated with degrees in chemistry and physics, and a master of divinity.

"I heard you speak several times when you returned to campus," I said. "We all looked up to you."

"Oh, you were there?" he said.

I explained my work in public relations, and how it led to improved relations between my clients and the black community. "I even have access to funds from Woolworth's designated to support black community relations initiatives," I said.

That last part caught Wyatt's attention.

"Have you met Dr. King?" he asked.

I explained that Sallie and I had met him briefly during his book signing in Harlem a few years earlier, but that was the extent of our interaction.

"You should come by our office today," Wyatt said. "We're just up the street, and Dr. King is there."

It was the invitation of a lifetime, and it was still hanging there when Mama's voice came to me: *Bobby, the best way to influence others is to be helpful.* She often talked about this in the context of the black church, which she rightly saw as our most powerful force for bringing social change. *Lean on the church,* Mama would say. *That's where you'll find people you can trust.*

With her voice in my ear, I shook the Reverend Walker's hand and told him we would be right over. I could not pay our check fast enough. Stanley and I flagged down the waiter, settled the bill, and walked the few blocks up the street to the headquarters of the Southern Christian Leadership Conference. The walk was short, but I was having trouble breathing because I knew this was a big moment. It was my chance to get involved in a great cause, one that might elevate the lives of millions of marginalized people. My people.

I prayed all the way there. *Lord, give me the strength to serve Your purpose.*

Wyatt greeted us at the front door and escorted us into Dr. King's office. He rose from his desk as if expecting important guests.

"Martin, this is the person I was telling you about," said Wyatt. "He is working with companies that might be willing to help us financially."

"I'm glad you are here, Mr. Brown. We need your help," said Dr. King. "We haven't got enough money or contacts with the business world."

I explained that it would be my honor to assist them, because their efforts to end racial inequality benefited me and all of my family and friends. Dr. King and Wyatt were spiritual men determined to drive societal change, but in this initial conversation they were pragmatic. They had bills to pay, and their organization was struggling hour-to-hour to meet expenses. They needed a lifeline.

I gave Wyatt my card and told him to contact me. Maybe I could help. He called the next day, and nearly every day over the next six or seven years.

Tall and taciturn, Wyatt was the disciplinarian and enforcer among King's lieutenants. Dr. King had brought him in to get the SCLC organized, and that he did. Although Wyatt had a scholarly manner, he was far more willing to confront his foes and antagonists than most ministers, and maybe even most prizefighters.

I was never as close to Dr. King as Wyatt was, but we certainly were good friends who respected and trusted each other. He considered my contacts in the business world to be an important asset, and I did my best to help him in every way.

There have been some attempts over the years to diminish the role of the Reverend Martin Luther King Jr. in the civil rights era. Some have claimed he was a mere figurehead. I can't understand that. I was there in Dr. King's public and private moments with the SCLC. Make no mistake, he was the lifeblood of the movement, he was our inspiration and our torch carrier as well as the chief strategist.

For many reasons—his intellect, his charisma, his skills as a communicator—Martin moved to the forefront, and everyone recognized his power as a leader early on. I was drawn to him for all of those reasons, but especially because we shared deep spiritual roots. We believed that we were all God's children, black and white, and that no man should subjugate another. We held the conviction that faith should be put into action. And in the years that followed, we would have plenty of opportunities to put that conviction to the test.

AFTER JOINING the SCLC board, I began working closely with Martin, Wyatt Walker, and their legal advisor Chauncey Eskridge, who also handled accounting matters for the SCLC and its foundation. They came to me when SCLC coffers were low and payrolls had to be met.

Wealthy entertainers like Harry Belafonte, Sidney Poitier, Ossie Davis, Mahalia Jackson, and Sammy Davis Jr. had been donating from their personal funds, and thousands of regular folks also contributed small amounts that added up over the years. Still, finances were always a problem for those in the movement. At one point, Martin had to cancel all SCLC credit cards because its bank accounts were in danger of running dry. We were constantly beating the bushes and passing the hat.

To help out, I arranged for financial assistance on behalf of many local civil rights groups, as well as individual freedom fighters. I solicited donations from several corporations. Many of America's top companies funded the civil rights movement to a greater extent than people realized, then or now.

I also found myself serving as a sounding board for the SCLC leadership, who thought my business connections could help them get other things done. I didn't participate in SCLC strategy sessions, however, because I didn't want to be in a position of planning demonstrations and protests against companies I was affiliated with.

My role was a humble one. Almost always I worked behind the scenes and out of the limelight. I didn't lead. I served, facilitated, and found common ground. I never pretended to be, nor did I aspire to be, the most important or powerful person in the room. I'd been taught from childhood that we all are created to serve a higher power: "Always be humble, and let God go first."

Mostly I kept the lines of communication open, and the money flowing. When civil rights leaders held massive meetings to organize protests or voter registration drives, someone had to foot the bill for their travel expenses, lodging, and meals. I took care of those costs many times, using funds passed to me by corporate and individual sources. I often carried as much as $8,000 to $10,000 in cash for emergencies, including paying bail money or for medical care.

My dual role, though precarious at times, provided a unique perspective on major events at a particularly tumultuous and dangerous time in our country's history. From 1960 through 1968, at least thirty-five blacks and whites—men, women, and children— became martyrs to the cause of civil rights, according to the Southern Poverty Law Center. Often I thought we were all headed for another civil war.

I thanked the Lord daily for being allowed to serve the cause of racial justice. I also asked God for guidance, because the fact was, I was winging it most of the time. Great men and women were struck down. But it always seemed that, in the darkest moments, God spoke to those with the power to bring change and said, "Enough. You are more alike than you are different. I did not create you to destroy each other."

There was one other service I provided for the foot soldiers in the civil rights movement, and I know it was warmly appreciated. Dr. King and other beneficiaries never got cold feet, thanks to me. You see, I kept them supplied with socks.

Martin liked to take off his shoes and put his feet up during informal meetings. I noticed one day that he had a hole in his sock. As a native of a renowned textile mill town, I was in a position to do something about that. My hometown was then the nation's center for hosiery manufacturers, and several of my friends owned textile factories that made socks. After seeing Dr. King's need, I went home and purchased several large cases of socks at a discount. From that point on, wherever I went, I always carried a few bundles to hand out to my friends in the movement.

On more than one occasion, I walked into a meeting and Dr.

King and his SCLC cofounder the Reverend Ralph Abernathy would smile, nod, and reach down to tug on their socks in thanks. My sock service was widely known within the movement. In fact, I just recently learned that the U.S. congressman John Lewis, a legendary civil rights advocate, claims to still have some "Bob Brown" stockings in his closet. I also provided my "sock treatments" to other SCLC clergymen, including Andy Young, Joseph Lowery, and Otis Moss, over the years.

AFTER I BEGAN working with the SCLC, I returned to High Point to relax and regroup as often as possible, but sometimes even at home I had no rest from the social upheaval. One night in late 1962, a group of about fifty young people, several local preachers, and a few doctors and other leading black citizens marched past my office on Washington Street, causing a commotion.

I had so much work to do, but I could not put aside the nagging thought that I ought to see what was going on in my community. High Point was still highly segregated, and it turned out that this protest was aimed at the local A&W Root Beer Drive-in, yet another place where a business welcomed our money but not our presence in the dining area.

The A&W was a favorite hangout of white teens in High Point, but we never felt comfortable there. I called Sallie and told her I wanted to check out the demonstration. She was a little reticent to join, but I told her several friends would be there too. Upon arrival, Sallie and I were glad to find a peaceful group assembling down the street from the drive-in.

Once the march began, there was shouting back and forth between marchers and hecklers. When we arrived at the drive-in, the owners asked police to arrest all of us for trespassing. The next thing we knew, Sallie and I were ordered into the same paddy wagons that I'd once kept busy with my arrests as a city patrolman.

Two white officers noticed me in the crowd. They were polite, but they indicated that there would be no special favors. Once we reached the station, they locked us up like everyone else. It might have been easier to accept being jailed in Mississippi or Alabama, but this was my hometown, where I'd fought to preserve law and order. I felt humiliated and angry over the injustice. All of us had been protesting peacefully. There was no need to haul us away.

For some reason, my anger triggered flashbacks to my days caddying at the local whites-only country club, where some of the members called me "nigger" and mocked me. I was seething. Sallie tried in vain to calm me.

"Robert, we'll be fine. They won't hold us for long."

Fortunately, I didn't have time to stew in those dark feelings. There was one advantage to being jailed in High Point. I had friends nearby who could come to the rescue. After about an hour our lawyer, Sam Chess (a boyhood friend who would become North Carolina's first black state superior court judge), came and bailed us out.

I felt belittled being arrested with my wife—our first and only trip to jail together—yet the experience also left me feeling as though I'd been fully baptized into the movement. Sallie was mortified by the experience: "Oh Robert, I don't know if I could ever do that again, that was so horrible."

I promised her that I'd never let such a thing happen again.

"We're going to fix this," I said. "We will keep fighting until we fix it."

After several meetings with city officials and concerned residents, we created the Citizens Steering Committee in High Point. We presented thirteen demands to the mayor's citizen advisory committee that included ending Jim Crow citywide, greater involvement of blacks in local government, and increased hiring opportunities in both the public and private sectors.

We moved a few mountains, and I managed to stay out of jail.

In fact, just a few years after I'd been arrested, High Point's Junior Chamber of Commerce named me the 1965 Outstanding Young Man in the community. I'd just turned thirty, so I still qualified as a young man, but this was the first time they'd given the award to a black person.

That told me something about High Point. I felt as though my love for the community and its people was justified; and I guess in some ways it was returned. The honor also gave me hope that most people eventually would do the right thing, given the opportunity to do it while saving face.

IN THE SPRING OF 1963, Dr. King and Wyatt Walker asked me to accompany them into one of their organization's primary battle-grounds: Birmingham, Alabama.

If Atlanta was home base for the champions of civil rights, Birmingham served as the main camp of their most violent enemies. Not every white person in this town was racist, of course. There were many white leaders who tried to find ways to end segregation peacefully. Yet racism flourished in its most vicious forms. Between 1957 and 1963, there were at least eighteen racial bombings there. The town had earned the nickname "Bombingham" because there had been so many explosives planted in black churches, businesses, and residential areas. There were more than fifty cross burnings during those years.

Birmingham's buses, restaurants, drinking fountains, fitting rooms, and restrooms remained segregated, even as other cities rolled back discriminatory practices and laws. City officials even shut down all city parks rather than obey a court order to allow black children to play in them.

Wyatt Walker and Dr. King and SCLC strategists Fred Shuttlesworth, Ralph Abernathy, Nelson Smith, and Andrew Young targeted Birmingham as ground zero in their campaign against entrenched racism. Their strategy for the city was code-named "Project C," with the "C" standing for "confrontation." As historians and others have noted, this was a meticulous plan that often disintegrated into chaos when faced with relentless opposition.

Project C kicked off on April 3, 1963, with sixty-five demonstrators descending on five segregated lunch counters in Birmingham. Four of those lunch counters, including Woolworth's, simply closed for the day when the protestors approached. A fourth, Britt's, remained open and summoned police, who arrested twenty-five demonstrators. The next day, police dogs were used to stifle another demonstration and more were arrested, bringing the total in jail to about 150, which was far more than those arrested during the Greensboro demonstrations.

Bull Connor, the city's hard-nosed public safety commissioner, was outraged at the protests. To put a stop to them, he secured a court injunction banning civil rights demonstrations. A deputy sheriff presented the court order to Dr. King and his lieutenants in the restaurant of the Gaston Motel (owned by local black business leader A. G. Gaston), where I was staying on the same wing as Dr. King and the Reverend Mr. Walker.

Martin immediately declared that the injunction was unconstitutional. He vowed to defy it. On Good Friday, April 12, 1963, Dr. King, Rev. Abernathy, and about fifty others were arrested and thrown in jail for staging a public demonstration without a permit. Martin was put in solitary confinement.

I was not among those arrested, so I joined in the effort to free them, which drew support from across the country. Entertainer Harry Belafonte, a major donor to the movement, came up with $50,000 to pay the bail of those who wanted out of jail.

Martin refused to bail out. He thought he could bring more attention to the cause by remaining inside. Several local ministers made a show of support by opening their churches to us, but others were critical of Dr. King, portraying him as an outside agitator and an extremist. Their criticism stung and angered Martin. On April 16, we learned that he was preparing a public response in his jail cell.

I was working with other SCLC members in our temporary office at the Gaston Motel when Martin's lawyers, Chauncey Eskridge and Clarence Jones, brought in a bunch of papers they'd smuggled out from the jail. Scrawled every which way, up and down on scraps of the *New York Times* and the *Birmingham News,* was Martin's handwriting. Other bits of text were on ripped-up grocery bags, and still others on sheets of toilet paper. The lawyers had stuffed the scraps in their coat pockets after Martin handed them over.

Wyatt, Andrew Young, Clarence Jones, and two or three others worked at deciphering what Martin had written in his cell. They'd pass the scraps back and forth, hoping that if one of them couldn't figure out what Martin had written, someone else would. Wyatt said Martin's writing looked like "chicken scratching," but the words were remarkably moving, just brilliant.

Martin had such an expansive mind and keen memory. He could pull together stories from the Bible and ancient history and philosophy, and relate them to what we were going through in Birmingham. We were all stressed beyond belief with the violence and bombs going off, so once the letter was strung together and we started reading it as a whole, many of us were overcome with emotion.

Those compiled scraps of chicken scratch would become one of Martin's most famous works, *Letter from Birmingham Jail.* As I read it back then, I was overwhelmed by the power of his words, which were the perfect response to the ministers who had criticized him as an extremist. The writing reflected the spiritual roots of his drive for social justice and racial equality.

"Was Jesus not an extremist for love," Dr. King wrote. "Love your enemies, bless them that curse you, do good to them that hate you, and pray for them which despitefully use you, and persecute you." Tears flowed and chills went up and down my spine as I read his words.

After staying in jail for a week, Martin and Ralph agreed to be bailed out, feeling that their time in prison had brought a great deal of attention to the cause. We were especially pleased that President John F. Kennedy had called Coretta Scott King to reassure her that Martin would not be harmed in jail.

But the battle in Birmingham was far from over. Each month in the spring of 1963, the violence escalated.

I attended a planning meeting for the Birmingham protests. The SCLC's project coordinator in Alabama was Rev. James Bevel, an aggressive young minister who pushed to recruit school-age children to the cause, in part because fewer adults were showing up. They could hardly be blamed. Many feared for their lives, or at least their livelihoods, if they were to be arrested and jailed.

Dr. King, Wyatt Walker, and the rest of the SCLC board worried that the entire national movement would lose momentum if we didn't keep pressuring the white establishment in Birmingham. The general consensus was that if the SCLC could bring down Jim Crow in this segregationist city, the rest of the South would follow. But we needed marchers, and the threat of police violence and arrests had made many wary of participating.

At this planning meeting, Rev. Bevel said he'd been speaking in local schools and talking to teens around town, and they were raring to go. Even younger kids in grade schools were excited about joining demonstrations, he said, noting that they were more enthusiastic than adults and would show up in bigger numbers.

Rev. Bevel made the point that young people were less likely to be mistreated or convicted of crimes and sent to prison. Wyatt Walker supported Bevel's plan. Dr. King and others voiced apprehension that the movement could be seriously damaged if young people were hurt or killed while demonstrating.

Martin believed children couldn't appreciate the risks of demonstrating in Birmingham, where racists felt empowered and protected by powerful segregationists like Bull Connor and Governor George Wallace. Rev. Bevel countered that anyone old enough to accept Christ was old enough to live their faith by fighting for justice.

I don't know if Martin or Wyatt ever gave formal approval of using young marchers, but when protestors began arriving on May 2 for the planned demonstration, the vast majority of them were teens and schoolchildren. Their youth didn't keep them out of jail. Local law enforcement began rounding them up right away, but they were quickly overwhelmed by the sheer numbers. Birmingham police had to bring in school buses to handle the six hundred or so they arrested. The young demonstrators filled the jails, so police had to use the fairgrounds to hold and process them.

The next day, even more young protestors showed up to continue the demonstration. At first they moved peacefully from the 16th Street Baptist Church toward City Hall, but just as they reached Kelly Ingram Park in the next block, they were met by an infuriated Bull Connor and his police force armed with billy clubs. They were backed up by German shepherd police dogs and powerful water cannons.

I was standing in Kelly Ingram Park when hell was unleashed. As Wyatt Walker and I entered the park, Wyatt noticed Connor's forces gathering to move against the kids marching. He warned me to stop just as the police began mowing down protestors with fire hoses fitted with special long-range nozzles capable of ripping the bricks off buildings and tearing the bark from trees.

"We'd better get out of the way of this. This is going to be a mess," Wyatt said. We hastily returned to the SCLC headquarters at another building owned by A. G. Gaston.

With our stomachs churning, we watched the violence from the second floor, standing in a stairwell that had walls of windows.

I saw boys and girls and adults knocked off their feet and sent tumbling down the street from the force of the powerful streams of pressurized water. Snarling police dogs attacked and dragged down demonstrators of all ages, ripping and shredding their clothing and biting their arms and legs.

Rev. Shuttlesworth was among those injured when hit by the hoses. He had to be hospitalized. The firemen and police officers had no remorse or compassion for the children or the adults. Cops chased kids down and beat them with billy clubs. I wanted to throw up, it was such a sickening sight, an unbelievable display of racial hatred.

Wyatt and I were both in tears by the end of it. We were all in a daze. The incredibly violent police response to peaceful protestors was one of the worst things I'd ever seen. Bull Connor and his henchmen were out of control. *Beat 'em. Kill 'em.* It seemed to make no difference that most of those they attacked were school kids doing nothing more than marching for social justice.

That was the world we lived in. In the face of such rage and cruelties, Andy Young, Dr. King, and others feared that protestors would seek retribution. They urged the demonstrators to refrain from throwing rocks and bricks, and to remain nonviolent.

The protests and the thuggish police response went on for nearly a week. Walking the streets in Birmingham in those days, I could taste the racial hatred like blood in my mouth. We were on alert everywhere we went, watching our backs and the shadows.

The protests became known as the Children's Crusade, and while we'd had our doubts about involving young people, we came to believe that God had ordained their presence. The violent response by the police, and their treatment of the teen protestors, outraged the world and finally brought offers of conciliation from the more sensible white leaders in Birmingham.

Even President Kennedy said he'd been sickened by front-page photos in the *New York Times* of a police dog attacking Walter

Gadsden, a young onlooker at the protests. JFK's brother U.S. Attorney General Robert F. Kennedy dispatched a team of Justice Department lawyers to Birmingham at the president's urging.

Dr. King provided them with a list of his demands, which they took to Birmingham's more conciliatory members of the Senior Citizens Committee on Tuesday, May 7. Our four demands consisted of the desegregation of all public facilities, equal job opportunities, the dropping of all charges against demonstrators, and the creation of a biracial committee to reopen city parks and other public areas that had been closed rather than desegregated.

The Justice Department negotiators worked from Tuesday through Thursday. They secretly moved between the Senior Citizens Committee members, led by business leader Edward Norton (the board chairman of Royal Crown Cola), and our local supporters, led by A. G. Gaston.

Mr. Gaston generally preferred to stay behind the scenes, but he became more publicly involved in the movement after the Birmingham police unleashed the dogs and power-hoses on our people. He took part in negotiations with city leaders and helped bring resolution after the violence. In the weeks and months that followed, Birmingham took down all WHITES ONLY signs, and integrated its schools and public buildings.

Even as meetings with civil leaders were under way, I was working the phones to raise funds to bail out all of those protestors jailed in Birmingham. We needed nearly $90,000 in cash. The SCLC received big donations from Harry Belafonte, Governor Nelson Rockefeller of New York, United Auto Workers, and Chase Manhattan Bank, which helped free all of those arrested.

Still, the most vehement foes of racial equality did not give up their old ways easily. The local leaders who sat down to negotiate with Dr. King were attacked by racists for "giving in" to him. These extremists who clung to Jim Crow and their hatred would lash out again and again before we prevailed.

———

ONCE WE BAILED everyone out, Dr. King said he had decided to return to Atlanta on Saturday morning. His father had asked him to preach at Ebenezer Baptist Church on that Sunday, so he could share his thoughts on what many were calling a historic victory for human rights in Birmingham.

After hearing that Martin was leaving Birmingham, I headed home too, on Friday, taking the opportunity to return earlier than planned to the relative peace of High Point. It had been an exhausting week, and I looked forward to relaxing with Sallie for the rest of the weekend.

But then, the very next day, Birmingham's unrelenting racists struck again. Around 10:45 p.m. on Saturday, May 11, 1963, the home and parsonage of Martin's brother, the Reverend A. D. King, was bombed. Fortunately, the explosion did not injure the minister or his wife and five children, though it did tear an eight-foot hole in their brick house.

I could not sleep after hearing about the bombing at A. D. King's home, so I was watching television when yet another special report flashed on the screen. Just before midnight, another explosion was triggered in Birmingham. This one was at the Gaston Motel, in the very wing where we had stayed the week before.

The bomb was placed near Room 30, Dr. King's usual room. He'd checked out only that same morning. The bombers apparently did not know that he'd left town earlier in the day; or maybe they wanted to make sure we would not return. The explosion all but blew off our entire wing of the hotel.

Several people were injured, though none were killed. I thought I'd been numbed to the violence brought against us, but this struck very close to home. If I had stayed behind, I most certainly would have been killed. My room was just a few doors down from Dr. King's.

I knew my grandmother watched the evening news, so I called her later that evening. She was still up, sitting in her favorite chair, waiting to hear from me, ready to console and encourage me, as always.

"Bobby, some people are so evil and godless, they have a lot to give an account for," she said. She thought it a shame that supposedly "Godly" men were hiding behind their faith to bring violence against blacks.

She was not the only one who felt that way. The bombings and the violence they provoked spurred President Kennedy to order three thousand federal troops into position near Birmingham. The president also threatened to federalize the Alabama National Guard. He made it clear that Dr. King's pact with Birmingham's white leaders had to be honored. His televised press conference the next evening seemed to restore sanity.

Yet on May 20 more than a thousand black students were suspended or expelled by the city's Board of Education for participating in the demonstrations. Dr. King returned to Birmingham to protest what he perceived as another attempt to provoke blacks. On May 22, a federal appeals judge declared the board's ruling illegal and ordered the students back to school.

Then, on May 23, another federal judge threw Bull Connor and his fellow commissioners out of office for good. For once, I felt as though all of the pain and suffering endured by the protestors had made a difference. The racists and haters had lost out. Their violence had resulted in positive steps toward lasting change. Dr. King, and all who'd directed their anger as a force for positive change, had persevered and emerged victorious.

Or so we hoped and prayed.

Chapter 7

VIOLENCE BEGETS VIOLENCE

B OB, I'M SORRY TO BE THE BEARER OF BAD NEWS, BUT THINGS have turned violent at the Woolworth's protest in Jackson; you'd better get back down there as soon as possible. It's on the news now."

The call came on the evening of May 28, 1963, from Bob Wood, executive vice president of the Carl Byoir public relations firm in New York City.

I turned on the evening news at Bob's urging and watched a sickening scene of racial fury play out. A network news show was broadcasting photos and film clips of whites dumping ketchup, mustard, and salt on the heads of black men and women seated at the whites-only Woolworth's lunch counter. The black protestors were dragged from stools and beaten on-camera.

This was exactly what I had been working to prevent for weeks. I'd just returned home from Jackson, where I had a dual mission. Woolworth's was my public relations client. I was also counseling civil rights leaders who staged the protests against the giant retailer in Jackson and across the South.

Racial tensions had been heating up in Jackson for weeks. Medgar Evers, the NAACP's field representative in Mississippi, had demanded the desegregation of all city departments, parks, pools, and other public facilities. But Jackson's mayor, Allen Thompson, initially rejected any talk of desegregation.

A confrontation seemed inevitable. My mission was to help avoid it, if possible. I'd gone to Jackson to advise Woolworth's local store managers about corporate policy on peacefully dealing with civil rights demonstrations—policy that I had written largely to protect the protestors from arrest.

Segregation was not a Woolworth's policy. The store had been following the laws of the state of Mississippi, as passed and enforced by segregationists. The police had sent a clear message: If Woolworth's opened lunch counters to blacks, local law enforcement could—and would—shut the store down.

Woolworth's officials believed they had to follow the state laws, so all I could do was set up company guidelines to avoid serious confrontations. I convinced Woolworth's that peaceful demonstrators should not be arrested or forcibly removed from the lunch counters. I also met with civil rights leaders Aaron Henry, Medgar Evers, and others. I assured them that Woolworth's corporate officials were doing all they could at the state and national levels to get rid of Jim Crow laws.

Once I had briefed both sides, I returned to High Point. The next day, we heard a widely disseminated report that Jackson's Mayor Thompson had agreed to desegregate public facilities and the city's departments. That seemed to be a great victory for civil rights leaders in Jackson. It had national repercussions as well, since Jackson was seen as a key battleground.

Then, just as our celebrations were beginning, the mayor publicly announced that he had *not* agreed to desegregate. His abrupt turnaround angered civil rights leaders. They had hoped for a peaceful, bloodless victory in Jackson.

I'd been monitoring the tense situation in Jackson from home when I received the call from Bob Wood of Carl Byoir. I watched the network news reports and then booked a flight back to Jackson the next day. Photos of the attacks on the Jackson protestors were featured on the front page of the *New York Times* and other newspapers on the airport newsstands.

As I made my way to Jackson, I felt caught up in a massive tide of racial conflict that often seemed beyond my capabilities to heal or control. As a black man, this was my fight, yet Woolworth's was my main client, the source of much of my income. My greatest loyalty was always to the freedom fighters and civil rights champions, but not everyone believed that I could be true to that cause and still do my job. Sometimes I wondered if it was possible myself.

BIRMINGHAM AND JACKSON were flash points for the civil rights movement in the spring of 1963. Between my business and my social activism, I seemed to have a foothold in most of them—and sometimes I seemed to be in up to my neck.

Jackson, Mississippi, was among those places where violence thwarted my efforts to build bridges. The attack on the Woolworth's demonstrators was likely committed by segregationists angry over our hard-won victory in Birmingham a few days earlier. It was a vicious assault.

A Tougaloo College professor who'd taken part in the sit-in was clubbed to the ground. Salt was poured into his head wound as he lay sprawled on the floor. A former city policeman kicked another demonstrator, Memphis Norman, in the face repeatedly until both were arrested by a real police officer. Photos of that beating were prominently displayed on the front pages of newspapers around the world.

Jackson was on the brink of a race war when I returned. Civil rights leaders were descending on the community from all over the country. Dr. King called for the president to issue an executive order declaring segregation unlawful everywhere. The White House said President Kennedy was busy with other things, which was a disappointment to those who'd hoped both Kennedys had finally committed to our cause. (On the evening of May 29, he celebrated his forty-sixth birthday on the presidential yacht; it would be his last.)

Executives at Woolworth's corporate office and at Carl Byoir were traumatized by what had happened at the lunch counter in Jackson. Like most people in the country, they were also fearful of where the violence might lead. Before I'd left home, I had a series of tense conversations with Bob Wood at Carl Byoir and E. F. Harrigan at Woolworth's. They feared the fallout would be horrendous, and their fears were justified. Similar demonstrations continued to plague Woolworth's stores around the country and at the company's New York headquarters, where protestors attempted to storm executive offices.

I had recommended to Harrigan and Wood that we issue public statements making it clear that Woolworth's corporate policy was to serve all people, but that Woolworth's hands were tied when state laws forced Jim Crow upon the company. I wanted to emphasize that Woolworth's officials supported peaceful demonstrations and wanted Jim Crow laws abolished.

Woolworth's officials felt like they were fighting a losing battle. There was little they could do to counter news photographs and film clips of blacks being beaten at their lunch counters, even if the company itself deplored racism, segregation, and the actions of those who attacked the demonstrators.

I remember thinking, *Will there ever be a time when blacks will know peace in this country? Is it even possible to have racial fairness and equal opportunity?*

Throughout this period, there were many reports of civil rights workers disappearing, forced off the roads, pounced on by mobs. I arrived in Jackson with my foot-long switchblade, the weapon I'd carried while working as an undercover federal narcotics agent, in my pants pocket. It was a hostile environment for any black person to enter.

I had usually worn a suit and tie while on the road for clients, which, for some reason, made those on both sides suspicious. Local segregationists often thought I was a civil rights lawyer, a reporter, or an "outside agitator" of some kind. After several close calls or challenges, I began dressing down to keep a lower profile, but Klan members and other racists monitored the airports and followed anyone who they thought might be working against their goals.

At the airport, I felt like a foreign diplomat entering a hostile country. There were small groups of rough-looking white guys gathered outside the airport. They seemed to be sizing me up. There weren't a whole lot of black folks traveling by air in those days. The racists figured any black man with the money to do that must be bad news.

Dr. Robert Smith, a local physician and civil rights activist who was about my age, met me at the Jackson airport. As soon as we pulled away from the curb at the terminal, a car with three white guys began following us.

"Don't get excited, but we're being followed," said Dr. Smith.

The car stayed behind us, matching the speed of ours on the highway to town. If we sped up, so did they. If we slowed, they did too. Maybe all they wanted to do was intimidate us, but we couldn't take that for granted.

The car followed us all the way to the inn where I was staying. We couldn't see much inside the car, but the vehicle idled outside as I entered the inn, and then drove off. Dr. Smith later said he hadn't wanted to leave me there, but there was no place else for me to go that late. Taking me to his home would have endangered his family.

I didn't like that these racist stalkers knew my location, particularly after the bombing of our wing at the Gaston Motel in Birmingham. Then again, I was relieved they hadn't shot at us or tried to run us off the road.

On the next day, March 31, the protests in Jackson escalated as the school year came to an end. Nearly six hundred grade school, high school, and college students joined a mass march that began at the Farish Street Baptist Church. The city had brought in hundreds of "special deputies," many of them virulent racists who joined local police and state troopers in surrounding the marchers near the church.

Cars circled the block, with passengers waving Confederate flags, as the marchers walked two-by-two on the sidewalks. As they proceeded, police and others blocked the street, beating the marchers with clubs, knocking them to the ground. There were so many arrested that police used garbage trucks to transport them to the state fairgrounds, where they were put in pens normally used for livestock.

On June 1, city police disregarded Woolworth's policies and arrested protestors at the store. Both Medgar Evers and NAACP executive director Roy Wilkins were among those taken into custody after Wilkins sat down at the lunch counter with television cameras capturing the scene.

Woolworth's officials went apoplectic at the arrests in their store. That wasn't supposed to happen, according to the policies I'd written, so I worked to get the charges dropped. It turned out that the local police had acted on their own in making the arrests.

We all knew the world was watching these events unfold. I was on the road for most of the month, in and out of Jackson and other Southern cities as I met with leaders eager to avoid similar problems. Then our worst fears were realized. An SCLC volunteer in Jackson, Annell Ponder, disappeared the day before a planned strategy session. She'd been on her way to Jackson from Georgia with a group of five young volunteers, including Fannie Lou Hamer, a field secretary for the Student Nonviolent Coordinating Committee, who later became a good friend of mine.

They'd stopped in Winona, Mississippi, on June 9, and went into a bus stop restaurant, but were refused service. They then encountered a Mississippi State Highway patrolman who threatened them. One of their group tried to write down the license plate of the trooper's car. A police chief also arrived and the activists were arrested. While jailed for three days, they were severely beaten, assaulted, and stripped of their clothing. Most of them, including Fannie Lou Hamer, who became a legendary and courageous activist, carried scars and suffered medical problems for the rest of their lives.

The situation only deteriorated from there. On June 12, the NAACP's local leader, Medgar Evers, was gunned down in the driveway of his Jackson home. He'd been shot in the back with a deer rifle as he carried some NAACP sweatshirts into the house for his three children.

The sweatshirts said JIM CROW MUST GO. Medgar had been encouraging blacks to boycott white-owned stores and to take part in protests, but also to be careful about confrontations. He'd been a courageous leader, a true intellectual, and a man of conscience who was devoted to the fight for human rights.

Medgar became one of the first martyrs of the civil rights movement. His murder both infuriated and reenergized its champions. Hundreds of people demonstrated around the country following his death, and President Kennedy finally asked Congress for a comprehensive civil rights bill.

The Civil Rights Act of 1964, which outlawed segregation in all of its forms, was signed into law the next year by his successor, President Lyndon Johnson.

LIKE MEDGAR EVERS, most of my fellow civil rights warriors had grown up in churchgoing families. We knew the Bible and its teachings, and we forged strong spiritual bonds. We prayed every day that God would give us the strength to continue.

There was another bond we shared, one that might seem contradictory: rage. Every day, often several times a day, we were cursed, shunned, spit upon, and showered with racial epithets.

Store clerks refused to wait on us, or shadowed us to make sure we didn't steal anything. Restaurants made us come in through the back door. They took our money, but then wouldn't allow us to sit down and eat our food.

Because of this, many of us harbored deep reserves of anger that we struggled to control. Usually our faith saw us through, but the rage was always there. We learned to take that fire inside and use it to forge wills of iron. We needed to be stronger than our unrelenting enemies, who held all of the power.

Today, blacks talk about racial profiling and being arrested for DWB, "driving while black." It was far worse back then. They didn't ask you to "step out of the car, sir." They shouted: "Get out of that car, boy!" And if you didn't move quickly enough, they'd have the gun upside your head in a hurry. Their goal was to get you to do or say something stupid, so they could make a case against you.

I was never beaten, though many of my friends were. I was jerked out of the car and pushed around some, standard treatment for a black person in those days. I always let the lawmen have their say. You couldn't win the argument, because they targeted you for no reason other than the color of your skin, and they had the law on their side.

Each small victory over Jim Crow seemed to heighten the tension and incite greater violence. We were poking a mean dog with a stick. Not a sleeping dog but a mean and cunning dog that bided its time and chose its place of attack. Some people simply disappeared and were never heard from again. Others showed up bruised and beaten after being gone for days. We were tracked and hunted like prey. My strategy during the 1960s and beyond was to "yes sir" and "no sir" them until they grew bored with me.

Not every racist wore a white sheet, of course. Some wore white collars. My corporate clients gave me access to white business and political leaders, but this didn't guarantee acceptance. I was usually the only black person present in the corporate meetings I attended during the 1960s. Most of the white executives had never interacted with a black man or black woman, either professionally or socially.

The CEOs and chairmen of the board were always cautious and self-controlled. It was rare for them to reveal any discomfort in my presence. That wasn't always the case with their subordinates. I'd also meet with regional vice presidents, executives, and managers around the country, and often they too weren't guarded about their racist sentiments, or their ignorance.

I'd hear comments like "Bob, I've never worked with anybody like you before. How'd you get this job?" Or "You aren't like any other Negro I've ever met." The comment that really set my teeth to grinding was "Bob, you are so well-spoken for a Negro."

We were as foreign as Tibetans to them. It wasn't unusual for my meetings or luncheons with white executives to turn into question-and-answer sessions in which they would pepper me about black culture, black consumer habits, or they'd ask me if I knew so-and-so, a black person whom they'd met somewhere in the world.

Most of the things that the white businessmen wanted to know about blacks carried a negative twist. They'd ask me about Dr. King's battle with the IRS, or about the rumors of his affairs outside his marriage. I generally responded to those inquiries by asking them if they were just as interested in reports about the tax problems or extramarital affairs of certain white celebrities, politicians, and entertainers.

In the early 1960s, I had an interesting encounter with a prospective client. Mr. Williams (as I'll call him) was an executive in charge of a Southern corporation. I'd suggested strategies he might use to ward off threatened black boycotts of his company's products. He agreed to meet with me, but then kept me waiting in an outer office for an hour or so.

Finally, he called me into his office.

"Robert, I read your stuff here, and you know, I think the Negro people ought to get their thing together. I just don't believe in all this stuff the niggers are doing today."

"Negro" was an accepted term in those days, but "nigger" certainly was not, and he knew it.

I didn't say anything when the offensive term slipped out. I continued to take notes as he talked about his support of Jim Crow laws. His arrogance and ignorance were all too common.

When he finally finished his rant, I stayed cool, but noted that using the word "nigger" was no longer acceptable.

"In fact, some Negroes might have become so angry that they'd be preparing to kill you right now," I said.

That seemed to grab his attention.

Mr. Williams had boasted of being a lifelong Christian, so I tried to connect with him on the level of faith.

"Don't Christians believe we are all God's children and deserve to be treated equally?" I asked. "Doesn't the Bible say there is neither Jew nor Greek, there is neither slave nor free, there is no male and female, for you are all one in Christ Jesus? How can you be a Christian and call another man a 'nigger'? If that is the sort of Christian you are, I want nothing to do with you and your business."

When I finished speaking, he hung his head.

"Robert, I really didn't mean it, I'm sorry. I'm very sorry. I won't ever do this again—not only in front of you, but never again, period. I am sorry and I am glad you put it the way you put it. I understand it better now than ever before, and I hope you will work with me. We will listen to what you have to say."

Based on that, I agreed to work with him and his company, and we went on to have a long association. He never again used racial slurs in my presence. His company hired and promoted blacks for the first time based on my recommendations.

This experience and similar encounters led to my creation of a booklet for my clients that outlined offensive words and racist behaviors unsuitable for the workplace—or any place. I did this well before the introduction of "diversity training," but the pamphlet became quite popular with my corporate clients, many of whom distributed hundreds of copies to employees.

I liked to think I was making a difference, but it was exhausting to deal with deeply embedded racism day in, day out. That's why my work with Dr. King and the SCLC was so important to me. I could do only so much on my own. I could see that Martin and his legions of followers had the power to change the world.

I ALWAYS TRIED to be a source of calm and a voice of reason in the fight for equality, but even my tolerance had its limits. In mid-September of 1963, I was at home in High Point, lazing around the house on a Sunday morning and getting ready to go to church, when I heard the first alarming reports on the radio. The 16th Street Baptist Church in Birmingham, Alabama, had been dynamited during a service.

We had held many meetings in that same church. I'd attended services there with other civil rights leaders. I tried to verify those initial news reports, but I couldn't reach anyone. Then the television newsmen confirmed the worst. Four little girls had been killed by the explosion while attending Sunday school in the church.

I'd been exposed to so much unimaginable violence already, but I damn near lost all control over this outrage. They murdered God's children in His own house, little girls in their Sunday school dresses. If that is not the definition of evil, I don't know what is.

News reports eventually provided the names of those killed. One of them, eleven-year-old Denise McNair, was the daughter of a friend, Chris McNair, a Birmingham photographer who'd often taken photos at SCLC events. I later spoke with Chris and offered to help him and his family in any way I could. Their grief was beyond my imagination.

I went to Birmingham the next day, Monday, September 16, 1963, to join thousands of mourners outside the devastated remains of the pretty little church. Some people were still going through the debris, picking up remnants here and there. Others were just standing, kneeling, or sprawled on the ground, weeping and praying.

We were all numb with sorrow. We'd all been so elated and rejuvenated by the recent March on Washington, where Dr. King had delivered his inspiring and powerful "I Have a Dream" speech. That had been little more than two weeks earlier, a moment that lifted the spirit, and then this insanity. Violence and hatred pierced our hearts once more.

Clearly, this was a major setback. That night, violence broke out all over the city of Birmingham as residents could not control their anguish and despair. They threw bricks and rocks, and set fire to buildings. Some of the blacks who lashed out were injured or killed.

Violence begets violence, as Dr. King often said. Yet there were those even within the SCLC who wanted to bring Birmingham to its knees. Martin feared an escalation, so he sent a telegram to President Kennedy asking for a meeting. He thought a racial holocaust could very well be ignited if the government didn't intervene to maintain peace.

This was an extremely volatile moment; some SCLC members proposed shutting down power companies and throwing themselves in the paths of trains and wheels of airplanes. Others called for creation of a nonviolent army to surround the state capitol in Montgomery until President Kennedy removed Alabama's racist governor, George Wallace, from office.

We walked through the broken bits and pieces of that beloved place of worship and felt as though all of our dreams of equality and freedom were scattered there on the ground too. All around me, normally controlled men and women were ready to strike back, talking of revenge and destruction. Usually in such situations, I tried to be a calming influence, the voice of reason over retribution. I can't say that was the case this time.

This was the worst evil I could imagine. Innocents had been slaughtered, including the child of a friend. *How will this ever end without more deaths? Will it ever end? What sort of world will be created for the children who survive? What is God's plan here?*

I prayed, as I'd learned in childhood. *Lord, help me understand, or at least help me accept what I cannot understand and put my trust in You.*

You could never convince me that God required the deaths of Denise McNair, Carole Robertson, Addie Mae Collins, and Cynthia Wesley before He would compel action to end the slaughter. But most historians say the church bombing, later attributed to four members of the Ku Klux Klan who planted more than fifteen sticks of dynamite in the building, was such an outrageous act of racial hatred that it forced our political leaders to act. It proved to be another big step in a journey that took far too long, and with far too many lost along the way. Tragically, the worst was yet to come.

Chapter 8

SECRET WEAPON

IN OUR PRIVATE CONVERSATIONS, THE REVEREND MARTIN Luther King Jr. often called me his secret weapon. Then he told everyone the same thing at the SCLC convention in the fall of 1967.

I was not present at that meeting, and you can only imagine my surprise when I learned that Dr. King mentioned me in his speech. I'd never wanted to call attention to what I was doing, in part because I didn't want to endanger my precarious position of trying to honestly serve my clients' best interests while advancing the cause of the civil rights movement.

I never betrayed the trust of either side. Instead, I worked to convince my corporate clients that racial equality and economic empowerment for black Americans was not only the right thing to do, but the smart *business* thing to do. The case I made wasn't just mine alone. Dr. King and other civil rights leaders were increasingly pushing the notion that the only way to create lasting social change and racial equality was by empowering minorities economically, and giving them a share in the American Dream.

Today when people think of the civil rights movement, they tend to focus on protest marches, sit-ins, and demonstrations. Those were certainly major offensives, but Dr. King and other forward-thinking leaders eventually chose to target the earnings of corporate America, by staging boycotts of their products when businesses refused to end discriminatory hiring and other racist practices. This strategy proved to be highly effective, and sometimes I played a supporting role by quietly working to bring both sides together.

The example cited by Dr. King in several of his speeches involved the A&P supermarket chain and one of its major suppliers, Sealtest Dairy, in Cleveland. The national brand's grocery goods— staples such as milk, cheese, ice cream—were extremely popular among black consumers. Yet, in a city that was 35 percent black, Sealtest's local plants had only 43 blacks among its 442 local employees. Martin and other civil rights leaders felt Sealtest was one of many companies reaping profits from black consumers while making only token efforts to hire and promote blacks.

The SCLC had created a division called "Operation Breadbasket," whose goal was to stage boycotts that would pressure major brands to hire and promote blacks, and also to support black communities and organizations just as they'd long done to show their appreciation to white customers. But as a national brand, Sealtest was not an easy target. The company had products in nearly every major grocery chain, as well as all the mom-and-pop groceries in the region.

Instead of trying to hit those scattered locations, the SCLC raised its sights and aimed at one of Sealtest's biggest distribution channels, the giant A&P grocery chain, which had stores in Cleveland's black neighborhoods.

When Sealtest officials didn't respond to initial requests for meetings, Operation Breadbasket distributed leaflets calling for boycotts of their products in black neighborhoods. Its leaders also went to every A&P store in those neighborhoods, promising that if their managers didn't remove Sealtest products from their shelves, pickets would be placed at their doors and blacks would refuse to shop there.

A&P was the largest grocery chain in the country at that time, but their stores operated on slim profit margins. They could not afford to lose black customers. Alarms went off at the chain's corporate headquarters when eighteen A&P stores were shut down by picketers on the first day of the boycott.

This is where I came in. The A&P supermarket chain had been one of my clients for about three years at that point. Their public relations firm, Carl Byoir & Associates, had brought me in because of my successes with Woolworth's. I'd been telling them that they needed to hire more black employees, train and promote more blacks to store managers, and sponsor events in the black community, but A&P was a big company and slow to change.

When the SCLC targeted their stores in Cleveland, I once again found myself serving as a bridge between a corporate client and the civil rights organization for which I was a board member and big supporter. I had friends on both sides of the table, people who believed in me and trusted me. A&P was paying for my services, and the SCLC knew that I believed in their cause: social justice and racial equality.

Dr. King described my role in this boycott in a speech titled "Where Do We Go from Here?," which he delivered on August 16, 1967, to the SCLC's tenth-anniversary convention in Atlanta. He noted that Operation Breadbasket convinced every A&P store "in the ghetto" to take Sealtest products off the shelves. Hundreds complied. Eighteen stores that refused to remove Sealtest products were shut down by protestors.

> The next day, Mr. A&P was calling on us, and Bob Brown, who is here on our board and who is a public relations man representing a number of firms, came in. They called him in because he worked for A&P, also; they didn't know he worked for us too.
>
> Bob Brown sat down with A&P, and they said, "Mr. Brown, what would you advise us to do?" And he said, "I would advise you to take Sealtest products off of all your counters."

A&P removed all Sealtest products from every store in Ohio the very next day. A day later, Sealtest representatives signed an agreement to hire more blacks in a deal that Dr. King said would create $500,000 in new income for the local black community. Sealtest also agreed to invest in black-owned financial institutions and to advertise in Cleveland's black-owned newspaper.

My role in this negotiation was to be the voice of reason for both sides. It made business sense for A&P to avoid shutdowns and demonstrations by pushing Sealtest to acknowledge and reward black consumers for their loyalty. Within two days, everyone was back in business. An extended boycott was avoided, and both sides walked away with substantial benefits that would pay off over the long term.

You can believe my phone started ringing shortly after this speech was delivered. I was overwhelmed when I first heard a recording of it, and really, I still am every time I read it or hear it. I had no idea Dr. King was putting me in the speech. Afterward, I teased him, saying, "Martin, you outed me, man! I can't hide anymore."

MARTIN AND I often talked about trying to enlist support from top executives who had the power to change the policies and attitudes in corporate America. We thought the real key to racial harmony was economic equality. We didn't want handouts; we wanted a level playing field for opportunities.

For years, protestors stormed the gates of discriminatory businesses and corporate headquarters. Martin and I discussed ways to accomplish our objectives from the inside out, instead.

Several months after Dr. King mentioned me in his SCLC convention speech, he and I had lunch in Atlanta to discuss those quieter approaches.

"Bob, you've been working with these businesspeople in New

York and around the country. I think it would be helpful, and we might achieve more, if we had private meetings with some of them," he suggested.

I agreed and offered to set up some meetings with some executives. Martin stressed that he wanted these to be very low-key and out of the public eye.

"This is the kind of meeting I'd rather have at our home than at a hotel or restaurant," he said.

That meant he had to check with the boss at home, Coretta, which he promptly did. After Martin sent me dates and times that worked out for them, I reached out to a contact at one of my biggest and most influential clients, the National Biscuit Company, now better known as Nabisco.

Nabisco owned large bakeries in Atlanta and elsewhere that civil rights groups frequently targeted. The company actually had blacks in a few key positions, but many of their production facilities, including their bakeries in Atlanta, were plagued with racial conflict and discriminatory practices in promotions and wages.

My job was to help the company do better in serving blacks in those areas. I suggested that Nabisco's senior executive Roy Kelly and future CEO Bob Schaeberle have an informal meeting with Dr. King so they could get to know and understand each other. They loved the idea.

The meeting was held two weeks later at Dr. King's home. Coretta made little snacks, and we sat at their dining room table for more than two hours. Martin asked the Nabisco executives to hire and promote more blacks, pay them higher wages, and create training programs for young people. He also encouraged Nabisco to support organizations within the black community as a method for building brand loyalty across the country.

Back then, asking major brands to support black organizations, schools, and churches was seen as "blackmail" by some critics of the tactic, but it became a popular strategy over time. Today many major brands like Nike, Coca-Cola, Procter & Gamble, and McDonald's support black organizations because they see the wisdom of building goodwill with black consumers, who are known for their fierce brand loyalty.

Nabisco had serious racial issues in its Atlanta bakeries and elsewhere, but Dr. King and I felt the executives were sincere about wanting to do better. We believed this was the future of the civil rights movement, because economic empowerment benefited all parties. Creating more jobs and encouraging entrepreneurship was much better than providing handouts that kept the poorest Americans dependent on government welfare or subsidized housing. This strategy provided motivation and opportunities for minorities to buy into the American Dream.

I believed at the time that we were moving into a new era of equal opportunity. Dr. King would have been its senior statesman, a champion of all people dedicated to positive social change and the greater good. Tragically, my friend, who had given so much of his life to the greater good, was struck down before he could see all of his sacrifices and suffering help to change the world.

While most of us thought economic empowerment was the future of the civil rights movement in the United States, Dr. King felt there were still major obstacles to be overcome in the fight against racial injustice, especially the drafting and deployment of blacks in the war in Vietnam. He considered it to be an immoral war and, like many, he believed that blacks were being drafted and sent into battle zones in disproportionate numbers. In his speeches, he promised to do whatever he could to defeat President Lyndon Johnson in the upcoming election, because Johnson had vowed to send in more troops.

Martin had always kept his anger under control and channeled it for positive action, but he found this war to be such a travesty that he could barely contain his rage. His mood darkened whenever the subject came up. These were dangerous times for prominent civil rights voices. We'd already lost Medgar Evers, President John F. Kennedy, and Malcolm X to assassins, and Martin had already had several close calls after attempts on his life.

On April 4, 1968, I returned to Atlanta at Dr. King's request for discussions on creating corporate sponsorships of antipoverty and desegregation programs for blacks in poor communities. Martin was flying in from Memphis, where he'd been dealing with an increasingly volatile situation.

Memphis had been in turmoil for months because of a strike by the sanitation workers in response to a long history of dangerous working conditions, low wages, and abuse of black employees. Martin believed his presence could help keep Memphis from exploding into violence again. On the night of April 3, he gave his famous "Mountaintop" speech at a black Pentecostal church in town, offering words that proved eerily, and sadly, prophetic:

> Like anybody, I would like to live a long life—longevity has its place. But I'm not concerned about that now . . . I've seen the Promised Land. I may not get there with you. But I want you to know tonight that we, as a people, will get to the Promised Land.

The speech moved many to tears. It was the talk of Atlanta when I arrived there the next day and went to the SCLC's headquarters for my meeting with Dr. King.

I took a seat in the waiting room and was there for an hour or so before Dora McDonald, Martin's secretary and assistant, came out and told me that Dr. King had just called and apologized. He had to remain in Memphis because of the intensity of the situation there.

Dora offered his apologies and said he promised to get in touch with me the following week. I was disappointed, but I knew Martin felt our people in Memphis needed him there to keep things under control. I decided to catch the first flight back home to High Point. I bid Dora goodbye and took a taxi to the Atlanta airport.

The soonest flight I could catch was to Charlotte, so I flew there with plans to rent a car and drive the seventy-five miles to High Point. But when I arrived in the terminal of the Charlotte airport later that day, I sensed something was terribly wrong. Men and women were distraught. Most seemed terrified and were openly weeping. Black folks especially appeared to be grieving, or angry, or both.

At first I thought there'd been another bombing, or a tornado or something in the area. The strange thing was that nobody would talk to me when I asked what was wrong.

I didn't have any luggage. So I headed to the rental car counter. On my way, I saw a black skycap who had a grim look on his face.

"What in the world is going on here?" I asked.

"What's wrong with you, man? Don't you know they just killed Dr. King?" he said.

I heard my own voice moaning: "No. No. No." Tears blinded me.

I went to the pay phone and called Sallie.

"Robert, where on earth are you? Dr. King has been killed and everybody is trying to find you."

She said that rioting was already under way around the country, and that even High Point was in turmoil. Angry young people were gathering on Washington Street. Local preachers were calling for my help. SCLC leaders and members of Martin's family were also trying to reach me.

I promised Sallie that I'd head home from Charlotte as quickly as I could. I was an emotional wreck. I rented a car and wept as I drove, listening in disbelief to radio reports saying Martin had been assassinated. There were frequent interruptions of the newscast by reports of rioting.

Radio reporters said blacks were rioting in New York, Washington, Atlanta, Chicago, and other urban areas. You could hear their shouts in the background. The anger in their voices was alarming. It seemed like our entire nation was being ripped apart. It was a terrible, terrible, terrible time.

When I finally drove up to our house in High Point, there were cars parked all over, in our driveway, the yard, and on the street. Friends and community leaders had gathered to meet me and to console us. I walked in and grabbed Sallie and hugged her, and we both sobbed until we couldn't breathe.

While our house was draped in grief over Martin's murder, the demonstrations raged nearby. Protestors had threatened to burn down the town. They'd already set fire to some old empty warehouses and a few other buildings near downtown.

We were all grief-stricken and confused. Several asked me what we could do to stop the rioting. I told them that this violence and destruction was not what Martin would want. He gave his life for nonviolence, and here we had people in the street burning and pillaging and doing just the opposite of what he'd preached.

I felt a responsibility to my friend, to his memory, and to my community. I thought it might help if some of us who knew Martin reached out and talked to those bent on destruction. So I called other black leaders around town, ministers and businessmen and politicians, and asked them to meet me in High Point's trouble spots. We walked the streets, trying to calm groups of rioters until two or three in the morning.

Around 6 a.m., Dora McDonald called me from Atlanta and said that Coretta wanted me to come back. Governor Nelson Rockefeller of New York had sent a personal plane to Atlanta to take Mrs. King and other family members to Memphis to pick up Martin's body. Coretta wanted me to accompany her on the plane.

I flew to Atlanta and met the family at the airport. Most of those aboard the plane were weeping. Coretta and her children rode in the front. I sat near them and next to the actor and activist

Ossie Davis. Harry Belafonte and other prominent supporters and friends were also onboard. We found it difficult to speak during that somber ride. We just tried to calm our minds with prayer.

When we arrived in Memphis, we met with the garbage workers' union leadership. They wanted to march, but Mrs. King was very uneasy about marching at that point. She had her young children and other family and friends with her.

I was a few feet away when Coretta turned and asked if we should march. I spoke up and said, "We should have a short march, and then return immediately to the airport with Dr. King's body."

Everyone agreed to that. Martin's young lieutenants, Andy Young and Jesse Jackson, had organized a march in Memphis. We participated even though there were persistent threats of violence. At that point, I didn't care if someone took shots at us.

I was angry, hurt, disillusioned, bitter. And yet I also felt a creeping numbness, as if my body was shutting down from shock. They had murdered my friend, a substantial man, a great leader who had the power to bring us all together, if only they'd given him the chance.

Martin had raised new levels of expectation and hope in America and around the world. I felt that hope had been taken away from us. It takes a lot to control the level of anger raging inside in such moments. I wanted to lash out, then and many times later.

As always, my grandmother came to me when I was on the edge of losing control. She had dealt with discrimination, racism, and adversity all her life. She never lost her cool. She prayed for those who tried to hurt her. Just thinking about her calmed me.

In the days following Martin's murder, I tried to do what I knew my friend would have wanted me to do. I counseled those who wanted to lash out, telling them violence only brings more violence. Not everyone was receptive to my advice. A few of the rioters I talked to were veterans of Vietnam and Korea. They said they'd been trained to kill by the government, and that they wanted to use their training to strike back.

I reminded them that when the Nazi sympathizer had struck Dr. King onstage at the SCLC convention, he did not strike back. Instead, he prayed for that man. Martin knew there was more power in his way. Above all, he knew the real power was in God's hands.

His killers had either been afraid of that, or ignorant of its truth. We knew that his effectiveness as a leader made him a target, and that the simple racists were not his greatest threat. Those of us around Dr. King were well aware that the FBI had monitored our activities for years. We always assumed that our hotel rooms and telephones were bugged. It was widely understood that there were informers planted inside the civil rights movement. Some of them have been identified in the years since, while others never were.

Early in my involvement with Martin, I received a warning of sorts from my associates at the Carl Byoir agency in New York. I'd just returned from a meeting in Miami, at the newly built Sheraton Towers, with Martin and other leaders.

This was a rare gathering in which everyone relaxed and partied. The libations flowed. We'd been on the road constantly, often in hostile and dangerous areas, working day and night. Everyone needed to cut loose. We had a bunch of suites and everyone roamed from one to the next, drinking and carrying on. There were a lot of jokes and some serious trash-talking about the FBI and their surveillance.

A few weeks after this event, I was having lunch with Byoir's executive vice president Bob Wood in New York. He offered what seemed like an odd statement: "You know, Bob, our tentacles reach out to different places in a lot of ways, and when you go to meetings with Dr. King you should be very careful of what you say, because there is surveillance."

I shrugged it off at first, thinking he was just giving me a general warning, but then he was more specific. "When you were in Miami, there were a lot of things said . . ." He then repeated word-for-word many of the comments made, including conversations conducted in my hotel suite.

I never asked him where his information came from. Byoir had hundreds of employees and some of them were former FBI agents, so I had a pretty good idea where Bob was getting his information. But in that moment, I just told Bob I was grateful to be made aware of the surveillance. He was trying to look out for me. He knew I was in a tricky position as a black man working within the movement while also representing many major corporations.

One of the things Bob said was that I should be careful about what information I shared about my clients with civil rights activists. He said our corporate clients would not be happy if they thought they were being put in a "trick bag" by someone on the payroll. I told him that I appreciated the warnings.

From that point on, I was extra careful. We all felt the pressure of scrutiny and the presence of danger in those years. A few months before Martin was killed, we had an SCLC board meeting in Richmond, Virginia, in which we talked about all of the threats he'd been getting. Martin talked as though he felt it was almost inevitable that he would become a martyr to the cause.

"If dying is the price I have to pay in the fight for freedom, then I will gladly pay it," Dr. King said.

Martin went so far as to offer his choice for a successor, selecting the Reverend Ralph Abernathy to lead the SCLC if he was killed. The mood turned very dark that afternoon. We were all fighting to control our emotions as he spoke. Daddy King, Martin's father, was sitting next to me, and he broke down sobbing. I comforted him and helped him get up. He kept saying loudly, "Please, Martin. Please, Martin. I can't take it."

Dr. King motioned for me to assist his father. I helped him walk out of the meeting. When we got outside, I asked: "Are you okay?"

"Bob, I can't stand it when Martin starts talking like that, all types of things go through me. I can't handle it. I don't want to see my son killed."

The Reverend Ralph Abernathy did take over after Dr. King was murdered. He proved a dedicated and courageous man, who had to step in at a very difficult stage. Some of Dr. King's other top aides challenged Rev. Abernathy's leadership and feuded among themselves. The SCLC also faced a decline in membership and financial troubles, struggling to continue its work without its charismatic founding leader.

Rev. Abernathy moved forward with Martin's plan for a Poor People's Campaign in Washington, DC, which Dr. King had envisioned as a major push for economic empowerment and social justice. It kicked off on May 12, 1968, with Coretta Scott King leading thousands of women in a Mother's Day march. The next day, thousands more participants began setting up Resurrection City, a temporary settlement of canvas tents and plywood shacks on the Washington Mall.

While this much earlier version of the Occupy movement brought international attention to the plight of the poor, it suffered from bad planning and a lack of supplies. The camp and its occupants were plagued with monsoon rains and intense heat. Resurrection City and the entire campaign struggled to present a unified theme. Then, once again, violence struck.

We had not even begun to recover from Dr. King's death when our spirits were dragged to the depths once more by yet another assassination, of yet another hopeful and unifying person I'd grown to admire and respect. This time it was Robert Kennedy, whom I'd spoken to at Martin's funeral a month earlier. He was shot by a twenty-two-year-old Palestinian just as he was celebrating his win in the California presidential primary.

The murders of Martin and John and Bobby left me and many others feeling lost and without direction. The warriors of the civil rights era had been pushing for social change from the outside for so long; I now began to think more of us needed to be on the inside.

Sometimes you have to be prepared to change your tactics. You may have successes, and the civil rights warriors certainly did, but if you lose your footing you may need to adjust and find a new way forward. I'd seen what corporate America and political leaders could do to accelerate societal change. They had the power to do what needed to be done without a lot of debate. They simply lacked consistent levels of motivation.

As the 1960s drew to a close, I began to think more about working from the inside out, rather than the outside in. I remained active in the SCLC and stayed in touch with many of the leaders, including Mrs. King. But my life was to take an unusual turn.

Unexpected events and opportunities would position me on the inside of the American power structure to a degree I never could have imagined. I quickly learned, however, that being the man inside brought its own challenges, frustrations, and dangers.

PART THREE

Chapter 9

CROSSING THE POLITICAL DIVIDE

ON THE NIGHT BEFORE DR. KING'S FUNERAL, I'D BEEN PART of a group of SCLC leaders who met privately with Bobby Kennedy. We'd all been impressed with his commitment to social justice. We had great hopes for his presidential run. After he was killed, many of us felt lost. I certainly did.

Most black Democrats shifted their support to Vice President Hubert Humphrey, whom I liked personally, but I had trouble working up any enthusiasm for his candidacy. I feared that his plans for addressing poverty would only create greater dependence on government handouts. I preferred an approach that created jobs and supported those striving to become self-sufficient.

I did do some campaign work and fund-raising for Humphrey, but I was on autopilot. In some ways, I felt that Humphrey's people—and most of the Democratic party leadership—were taking blacks for granted. They assumed we would support any candidate they put on the podium.

The chaos of the Democratic National Convention in Chicago that year also left me concerned about where my party was headed. Police beat antiwar demonstrators in the street. I couldn't help but wonder what Martin and Bobby would have thought of that. The whole country seemed to have lost its bearings.

As unhappy as I was with the Democratic leadership, I'd never thought of crossing over to the Republican side until I crossed a street in New York City one day and ran into Ted Brown, a longtime friend of Dr. King's. Ted was an international activist who joined South Africa's anti-apartheid movement long before other African Americans got involved. Ted was in New York that day with another guy I knew and respected: Clarence Townes, a business leader and bank director from Richmond, Virginia.

We stopped to chat, and I was surprised to learn that Clarence was working as an assistant to Ray Bliss, chairman of the Republican National Committee.

"Republican?" I asked, feigning shock.

Ted laughed and explained that he was involved with Richard Nixon's presidential campaign, too. "In fact, I've been trying to reach you to see if you might be interested in doing some work for them," he said.

I thought he was joking, but Ted reminded me that even Dr. King himself had been leaning toward the Republican Party candidates before President Johnson had decided not to run for a second term. Martin had become deeply disenchanted with Johnson's refusal to pull American troops out of Vietnam.

Still, Nixon was an enigma to me. I didn't have much feel for his stand on civil rights matters or ending the Vietnam War. He'd seemed evasive and noncommittal on those two key topics. So far, he had shown few of his cards.

My impression was that Nixon would do whatever was politically expedient. I told Ted and Clarence my concerns and misgivings about their candidate. They invited me to have a drink and continue our discussion. We walked to the Summit Hotel on Lexington Avenue and took a table in the restaurant.

There, my acquaintances continued their pitch for Nixon's candidacy. They noted that Nixon had grown up in the Quaker faith and was sympathetic to those on the margins of society. They said the candidate resented intellectuals and the privileged class, because he'd come from a poor background and had to fight for everything he'd achieved.

"He identifies with the underprivileged and the poor," they said. "The Quakers believe we should all help people in need."

These guys were good. They knew I'd attended a Quaker school as a boy, so they were definitely playing that card. They made the case that Nixon didn't believe in welfare handouts, but that he did believe in a form of "practical liberalism."

I felt torn between loyalty to my Democrat friends in the civil rights movement and my sense that we were about to enter a new stage in which government policy, not demonstrations and protests, would lead social change. I feared that too many Democrats favored welfare programs over more substantial things, like equal access to education and black economic development.

Maybe Nixon and his people could make things happen. Something had to be done. Blacks were falling deeper into poverty. Liberal programs had poured billions into the ghettos, but things were only getting worse.

They were definitely pushing my buttons. I respected them. I decided that it wouldn't hurt to have a closer look.

"I could work for you one day a week as a paid consultant, but I can't promise you more than that," I said. "I need to know more about the man you are backing before I'd commit anything further."

"We will get a contract to you tomorrow," Clarence said.

IF WORD GOT AROUND I that was working with Nixon's campaign, I knew there would be a backlash. At that point, only a few prominent blacks had dared to publicly support Nixon's candidacy.

I should have known Nixon's campaign staff would try to draw me into a greater commitment once they had me under contract. Within a couple weeks, they'd wrangled me into boarding the campaign train as a media liaison and troubleshooter. The fact that I was a card-carrying Democrat didn't seem to matter. They saw me as someone who could help them make inroads with black voters.

I had to admit that Nixon had a well-organized and disciplined army working for his campaign. His events started on time and ended on time. The balloons fell and the cheers went up exactly as planned. Credit for the campaign's military precision went to H. R. "Bob" Haldeman, a former New York advertising executive. He'd been brought on to remake Nixon's aloof image and sell him to voters as a global visionary and principled man of the people.

There was something reassuring about being part of a disciplined operation during such a tumultuous period, especially after all those chaotic years working with civil rights organizations. Still, my assignment in his campaign was a difficult one. Nixon had received about 30 percent of the black vote in his losing 1960 presidential campaign against JFK. His private polling indicated even less black support was likely in this campaign, due to increased antiwar sentiments.

Republicans were hoping Nixon would receive at least 12 percent of the black vote this time around, but a black reporter in Cleveland summed up the odds when he told Nixon point-blank: "The Negroes are a little afraid of you."

Many in Nixon's camp had written off black voters entirely, so my assignment was seen as a bit of a no-win mission. Then again, expectations were so low that the candidate was bound to be grateful for anything I accomplished.

While my primary job was to make inroads with black voters, I was also part of a team assigned to protect Nixon from antiwar protestors, who'd proven to be nearly as well organized and efficient as Nixon's own team. I usually went into each campaign stop two or three days ahead of the candidate to make sure arrangements were set, and that he had limited exposure to hostile crowds. I also identified any potential leaders and organizations for financial and campaign volunteer support.

In Rochester, New York, antiwar protestors had disrupted a

Humphrey appearance a week earlier. Nixon's campaign people did not want that to happen to him, so I arrived four days ahead of the candidate to see what I could figure out. Local ministers and community leaders told me the key to keeping the peace was "the Brass brothers."

Benny Brass and his brother were former gang leaders who'd become community activists for the poor. The Brass brothers played both ends against the middle. They had positive and negative sides. My only interest was to make sure they did not derail Nixon supporters as they had done with the Humphrey team.

The Brass brothers had already checked me out and decided to trust me. They said they'd control the crowds for Nixon's appearance. They also made it clear that they would hold me to my word if he won the White House.

The Brass brothers kept the lid on. They even had black crowds at the airport to greet and cheer for Nixon when he arrived. Their efforts did not go unrewarded.

My efforts in Rochester were rewarded too. In the eyes of Nixon's campaign managers, I'd accomplished the impossible. After the campaign appearance, I was called to a hotel room where I met with campaign manager Bob Finch, Nixon's lieutenant governor in California, who later became secretary of the Department of Health, Education, and Welfare.

"The old man thinks you should be closer to the heart of the campaign," Finch said. "He wants to let you know he appreciates what you did, and he wants you to start traveling with us on a day-to-day basis."

The campaign wanted me to help handle the media and other duties on a whistle-stop train tour that would produce more positive results and enhance the voter turnout on Election Day.

I knew that taking this job would signal that I'd officially crossed over to the dark side in the eyes of my black Democrat

friends. Yet my instincts told me that I'd been on the outside, looking in to the sources of true power, for long enough. Nixon was
still something of a mystery to me. We'd met a few times and he
was warm enough, despite his reputation for being an introvert. I'd
heard him speak convincingly on his desire to help minorities and
the poorest Americans.

The key to understanding him, I learned, was to acknowledge
his contradictory nature. Nixon always saw himself as the under-
dog, even when he held the most powerful position in the world. He
didn't trust many people, but he related well to other underdogs.

As later revelations from tape recordings and his own hand-
written notes revealed, Nixon was capable of great warmth as well
as utter ruthlessness. I was fortunate to be on his good side, and
to have his support throughout my association with him. He was
there for me even when he didn't have to be, and I tried to support
him as long as he didn't ask me to do anything contrary to my own
principles and values, which he never did. I supported and loved
him until his death.

DURING THE CIVIL RIGHTS campaign, I had developed skills as a
fund-raiser, but it had never been so easy back then as it was working for a Republican candidate for president. When I went on the
road for Nixon, his eager donors all but threw money at me to support his campaign. Frequently I'd get calls from my public relations clients asking if I would mind delivering their contributions
directly to the candidate.

I'd go to meetings and come back with five, ten, fifteen, twenty
thousand dollars in checks. Several top executives gave me checks
for as much as $10,000 each to support Nixon's candidacy. I also
collected donations from a lot of Democrats who liked Nixon but
didn't want it known that they'd contributed to him.

Nixon's people seemed to be astounded that a black man could raise that kind of money. They were impressed that I had so many contacts in the corporate world, and in the civil rights community too. During the campaign, Nixon's advisors asked me several times what sort of job I wanted in his administration if he won.

"I need to return to my wife and business in North Carolina. My firm has suffered in my absence, and I need to build up my client base," I told them. "But I'd be willing to open a Washington, DC, office if we could work out a consulting contract."

They were shocked that I wasn't interested in a White House job, but I was wary for good reasons. I still wanted to be closer to the center of power instead of on the outside looking in, and I thought my contacts within the Nixon team could help achieve that even if I wasn't working directly in his administration.

To be honest, I had an even deeper concern. Other blacks had served in the White House in previous administrations, only to be given few responsibilities and little power. I wasn't interested in a token job. I wanted to have the power to keep pushing for racial equality and economic empowerment in the black community— and I still needed to make a living.

As it turned out, Nixon wasn't interested in giving me a token job either. He narrowly defeated a late-charging Hubert Humphrey in the 1968 election. The new president realized that he needed to build his political base by reaching out more to Democrats and to black Americans. Apparently he saw me as someone who could help him build those bridges.

On the morning after the election, I received a telephone call in our room at the Waldorf Astoria Hotel in New York City. It was Bob Haldeman.

"The old man wants us to go to Key Biscayne and put the new government together," he said.

"I'm not going," I said. "I'm done. Sallie is here and we are going to rest for a few days. I haven't spent time with her in weeks, and I have to get back home and put my business back together so I can make some money."

Haldeman repeated that the president-elect wanted us to work on the transition together, and that he was sure Nixon would want me on his White House team. Again, I told him that I'd be happy to work with him as a consultant, but that I didn't want a government job, even in the White House.

"Well, I'm sure the old man will want to talk to you about that," Haldeman said.

After a few days of R&R with Sallie, I returned to my High Point office only to be bombarded with calls from Nixon's team. They had questions about things I'd worked on and contacts I'd made. And they called every day to tell me that Nixon wanted me on his White House staff.

One day in late November, Haldeman called me in High Point. His message was different this time: "The president-elect wants to see you," he said.

That sort of phone call doesn't come often in life. I figured it wouldn't hurt to talk to the man himself, just in case I needed a job reference down the road. I was already prepared to go to New York to meet with Woolworth's executives and my Carl Byoir contacts, so I told Haldeman that I'd stop by and talk with them the next day.

"Let me know as soon as you land at the airport," he said.

I agreed to do that, and then, when I hung up, Sallie wanted to know what Haldeman had called about. "Oh, they might want to have me do some consulting on the transition team, which I'm hoping could lead to more consulting once they are up and running, I said."

Sallie looked at me as though she wasn't buying that entirely. She always was hard to fool.

————

WHEN I ARRIVED at LaGuardia Airport the next morning, I called Haldeman as promised. "I just arrived and I'm on my way," I said.

"Call me when you get downstairs and I'll have them bring you right up," he replied.

I could tell from his tone that things were moving fast. He was Nixon's point man and he had a lot on his plate, so it was all the more interesting that he was taking the time to track me so closely. Nixon must have been on him to get me there; otherwise, he wouldn't have bothered.

Nixon's suite was on the thirty-ninth floor of the Pierre Hotel, offering a view of Central Park stripped of its leaves and flowers. The winter grass was brown, and the frozen ponds wore a slick sheen of ice. When I entered, Nixon was talking with his longtime friend and fellow attorney Bill Rogers, who would become secretary of state. Former U.S. attorney general Herbert Brownell Jr. was also in the room.

Nixon introduced me to them.

"I have to meet with Bob, he traveled with me and did great work during the campaign, and he is going to be one of my top assistants in the White House," he said.

Rogers and Brownell excused themselves. The president-elect didn't waste any more time with chitchat.

"Look, Bob, I need you on board," Nixon said.

I repeated my standard "thanks but no thanks" line.

Nixon refused to accept it.

"I need you full-time to help us pull everything together," Nixon said. "We don't have the White House staff set, or a Cabinet, and then I've got all of these boards and commissions to select. I need you here with me as a full-time assistant. Don't worry about your business. It will still be there when you are ready to return to it. I'll make certain of that."

He then dropped a few names just in case I didn't trust his clout.

"I know H. F. Johnson and Bob Kirkwood," he said, naming

the CEOs of Johnson Wax and Woolworth's. "They are both big supporters of mine, and they think a lot of you, too. They'll be there for you anytime you need work. They understand the importance of what we will be doing for this country."

Nixon was letting me know that he'd done his homework and that this wasn't just a job offer. It was a call to duty.

Nixon studied my face. He was a master at this sort of thing, applying flattery, leveraging power, calling in favors. Nixon knew he had me. After years pounding on the door to get the attention and cooperation of the white establishment, now they were inviting me inside.

"I'll try it for a year to help get your administration up and running," I told the president-elect. "Then I will go back to my business in High Point."

Nixon relaxed in his chair, but he continued his pitch. He talked about a man named Fred Morrow, the first black man who ever served as a special assistant to a president. Morrow had served under President Dwight Eisenhower when Nixon was his vice president, and Nixon lamented that Eisenhower had never given him much to do. Even blacks had dismissed him simply as "the Negro who sits by the door."

"You won't be like the man sitting by the door," Nixon said. "Fred was a good man, and what Ike did to him was a damned shame. He was competent, but they never gave him anything to do. He had no real responsibilities. You will. You will report only to me, and you will have complete authority to do what you think needs to be done for your people."

I told Nixon that I would leave in a heartbeat if I thought this job was just a token. I had a long list of things I wanted to accomplish—things that had been on the Reverend Martin Luther King Jr.'s agenda as well. I wanted access to the president, and his full support for whatever legitimate goals I set for him and his administration.

"Anytime you need to get to me, you can do it," he said.

Then the president-elect closed the deal. He told me I would be his "point man" for leading initiatives on black economic development across the country.

"There are certain things I want you to get to right away," he said. "I made that speech about black capitalism and it struck a chord. I don't know all the problems, but I know there are things that should be done. I want you to be the point man on that."

Nixon then touched on another area that I had not anticipated.

"I've been given a national security paper on major race problems in our military," he said. "There are things that have come out, and also some things that they've kept hidden. I want you to investigate these reports and decide what needs to be done. I want you to see to it that these things are taken care of, and whatever else you find that needs to be done. You'll have my full support."

This was a memorable, yet surreal, moment for a sickly child who'd grown up on the dirt streets on the poorest side of town. I could hear my grandmother's words, telling me to do good and to help others wherever I could. Certainly there were blacks who thought Nixon was evil. I'd had my ears burned more than once by friends and others who'd seen me on the campaign trail with him. Most had no faith that he'd do anything for black Americans. They thought he was insincere; a man obsessed with power more than a man with a vision for his country and all of the people in it.

That was not my experience, and even if he'd been the devil himself, I knew my own heart. I'd been able to influence Nixon and his team on the campaign trail by telling them what mattered with black voters. I thought I could do even more in the White House.

This was an opportunity to lift up others and to make good things happen on a scale I'd never imagined. This wasn't about me and what others might think of me. It was about doing something lasting and far-reaching with the incredible power of the presidency behind me.

Sure, there was a chance that Nixon wouldn't make good on his pledge. But if that happened, I knew how to buy a train ticket out of town. It was sure as hell worth a try.

I thanked Nixon and told him I'd join his transition team immediately. I left his hotel suite and found Bob Haldeman standing in the hall. He asked me to wait just a minute. He went inside, shutting the door, and emerged a few minutes later.

"Where are you going right now, Bob?" he asked.

I told him I was going back to the hotel to call Sallie and tell her that our life had just changed dramatically. "Then I'm returning to North Carolina to help her pack," I said.

"You can't leave today," Haldeman said. "The president wants to announce your appointment this evening or in the morning."

"You've got be kidding, I haven't even told my family yet," I replied. "My wife would think I'd lost my mind."

Before I knew it, he'd ducked back into Nixon's suite, leaving me in the hallway. I heard them talking rapidly, then Haldeman was back.

"Okay, Bob, you've got forty-eight hours," he said. "He wants to move quickly on this."

Chapter 10

CALLED TO SERVE

AFTER WALKING BACK TO MY HOTEL ROOM, THE FIRST THING I did was call my wife—my girlfriend since the fifth grade. This news could not wait.

"Hello?" she said.

"Sallie, I don't quite know how to tell you this, girl. You are not going to believe it when I do tell you."

"Stop it, Robert, just tell me!"

"It looks like we're moving to Washington, DC."

"Whatever for?" she asked. "What on earth is going on? Have you lost your mind? You just got home from campaigning for months!"

"Honey, the president-elect just offered me a job as his special assistant with full authority to make a whole range of things happen," I explained. "I'll be working at the White House. I told him I'd try it for just a year to help him out and get things on course. We'll just get an apartment in Washington and keep the house in High Point, and then we can return home to it."

"Oh my God, Robert, how can this be happening to us?"

I could tell it was sinking in. In a few minutes she'd be on the phone to her mother, all her relatives, and friends. *Robert has been asked to serve with the president in the White House!*

"Sallie?" I said.

"Yes, Robert?"

"This job will change our lives substantially, but we will be together and we will be just fine."

I am fairly certain she was dialing her mother before I hung up the phone.

I returned to North Carolina on the afternoon of Saturday, December 7, 1968. Sallie met me at the Greensboro airport with more than a dozen family and friends. We all hugged and laughed and cried together right there in the arrivals area. I suspect we may have consumed a whole lot of wine and champagne that night.

Sallie had an adventurous spirit, and she had always believed in me. She felt, bless her soul, that the rest of the world was finally recognizing my potential.

When I broke the news to my grandmother, my champion and my inspiration, tears soaked her sweet face. Then the realization hit her.

"Bobby, does that mean you are going to have to move?" Miss Nellie asked.

I told her we would keep our house in High Point and get a small apartment in Washington. I assured her that I'd be home for holidays and most weekends. She made me promise to call her every day.

Upon returning to New York, I checked in with Bob Haldeman. He told me that they'd set up a press conference for the next morning to announce my appointment. At the press conference, press secretary Ron Ziegler announced my appointment as one of seven special assistants to the president. My area of focus was to be domestic affairs with a particular concentration on minority issues.

As the first black man named to the new administration, the media considered me a curiosity, especially once word spread that I was still a registered Democrat and that I'd worked for the Kennedy and Humphrey campaigns. The wire services and other news media reported that my appointment was part of Nixon's concentrated effort to promote "black capitalism."

In many eyes, I was immediately marginalized as either a token or a house boy given a fancy title and a nice office. It didn't help that I was so young and largely unknown by political operatives in Washington, DC, but I saw no reason to apologize for that.

I fielded some odd questions in my first interviews with the press. It quickly became apparent that I was expected to serve as a spokesperson for all black Americans, and as a sort of translator for the national black experience, as if we all thought alike.

"How do black Americans feel about Nixon?"

"What do they want Nixon to do for them?"

The reporters at the press conference, all of whom were white, scanned my résumé, noting my background as a police officer, federal narcotics agent, civil rights activist, and public relations man. They didn't assume I was competent and ambitious. Instead, they wanted to know how I had managed to rise from a life of poverty in a small Southern town.

"How did you become so successful?" they asked repeatedly.

I understood their curiosity to a point, but Nixon had grown up in relative poverty too, as have many successful men and women. It was the color of my skin and the job in a Republican administration that threw everyone off. Like many black males of my era, I had grown accustomed to being underestimated. I planned to use that to my advantage.

I'D THOUGHT, rather naively, that black leaders in both political parties might be glad to have one of their own inside a Republican administration. It quickly became apparent, however, that I was neither Republican enough, Democrat enough, nor black enough to please many of my brothers.

My former civil rights cohort and the new SCLC leader, the Reverend Ralph Abernathy, had blasted Nixon immediately after the election results were tallied.

"Nixon offers no hope for the black man," he'd said.

Rev. Abernathy was well aware that Nixon had made me his

special assistant, so even though I knew Ralph was playing to his base, I found that a bit insulting. Anyone would've felt insecure stepping into Dr. King's role, and challenging the president is one way to look like a strong leader. My concern was that Rev. Abernathy was overplaying his hand so early in the new administration. I thought he should give Nixon—and me—the chance to demonstrate our commitment to the black community.

When I accepted the job, Nixon had basically told me that I was in charge of providing whatever I thought was needed for black America, and I intended to take full advantage of that.

My critics, however, mocked me as a dupe for believing Nixon was serious. I hadn't even begun to unpack the boxes in my office, Room 179 in the Executive Office Building, when my detractors started calling me the "White House Negro." One prominent black leader was quoted anonymously by a journalist as saying that I was just a token. He added that I probably had to go through twenty-five people just to talk to the president, when in fact I probably had more access to Nixon than 99 percent of the people in his administration.

As proof of my "token position," some critics noted that I'd been given an office in the Executive Office Building instead of in the White House. In truth, most of Nixon's special assistants were in the EO Building, located across a small alley from the White House. I had one of the biggest offices, and it was directly across the hall from "the old man" himself.

Nixon did most of his serious work in his hideaway office just across the hall from mine. He would go there to write, read, and contemplate strategies suggested by his team. Speechwriter David Gergen had an office down the hall. Other staff members with offices nearby included Herb Klein, head of the White House Office of Communications; Alan Greenspan, then a top economic advisor to the president; Nixon's hard-nosed special counsel Chuck Colson; and a secretive former "spook" who'd worked for the CIA, smoked a pipe, and tended to wear dark sunglasses even indoors. I didn't know him much. His name was E. Howard Hunt.

I had a spacious, high-ceilinged suite of offices with a reception area. It was one of the largest offices on the floor. I needed a lot of room because my areas of responsibility included just about anything going on related to black Americans: civil rights, black colleges, crime, job discrimination, welfare, poor black communities, race relations in the military, and black economic development.

From the day I started work on Nixon's staff, there were stacks of materials brought into my office for my review or approval. Mine was one of the biggest staffs for any assistant to the president. I kept three secretaries and three aides hopping at least sixteen hours a day.

President Nixon called me into his office when he wanted to talk about matters related to the black community, or if he was meeting with black leaders and wanted my input. I also set up meetings and provided him with background information to help him draft his remarks for domestic crisis meetings. Perhaps the most intense of those were called after the Kent State shootings, when we feared the entire country might blow up.

We socialized. too. Nixon and his wife, Pat, invited Sallie and me to join them at Camp David or the Western White House in San Clemente, California. I never thought to publicize my interactions with President Nixon, but maybe I should have. I'd been on the job just a few weeks when *Washingtonian* magazine quoted an unidentified source as saying I was "a boy sent to do a man's job." It seemed like a black man would automatically be seen as a token or an Uncle Tom if he worked on a Republican president's staff.

"You're just up there defending Whitey" was the comment I got from a St. Louis teen when I spoke at his high school.

The general attitude among blacks was that Nixon didn't give a damn about them, and neither did I, apparently. I'd rarely encountered such blind hatred and suspicion, even when facing racists during protests in Birmingham and Jackson. But I could handle the heat. When a reporter from the *New York Times* asked me about the flak I was taking for joining Nixon's White House staff, I gave an answer that would become my mantra for the next season of my life.

"Sure, I get my bumps for being here in the administration, but I'm here by choice," I told the *Times* reporter. "I've been in demonstrations and marches and gone to jail for participating. I know what it is to be black, have no shoes, and eat cold beans for breakfast. I don't care if someone calls me Uncle Tom . . . Who are they to say that my way is wrong and theirs is right? Results are the only things that count."

Still, when the Knight Ridder newspaper chain ran a story claiming, among other things, that I had no political support and that I was anti-union, I worried about being cut from the White House staff. This was early in the administration, and I wouldn't have blamed Nixon for thinking that I might be a liability he couldn't afford.

The day after the story appeared in newspapers around the country, President Nixon's secretary, Rose Mary Woods, buzzed me on the staff intercom.

"The president and Mrs. Nixon would like you to join them for dinner tonight at the White House," she said.

I told Rose Mary that Sallie and I were free. But given the heat I was taking in the media, I didn't see this invitation as good news.

He wants to let me down easily, I thought. *This is it. He's cutting me loose.* I feared that Nixon was going to say, "It's been good to know you, and I'm sorry but your services will no longer be needed."

I tried not to reveal my concerns to Sallie when I picked her up and brought her to the White House that night. There were only two tables of people, most of whom were among the president's closest friends and confidants. Rose Mary Woods was there. She'd been with Nixon forever and she talked to him more like a wife than a secretary. She was known for addressing the president of the United States without the usual formality. I can still hear her saying, "Well dammit, Dick . . ."

Attorney General John Mitchell, another high-profile figure in the Nixon administration, was also there with his wife, Martha. Sallie was glad because she and Martha, who'd grown up in Pine Bluff, Arkansas, got along very well. They could chat for hours.

The president's close friend, HEW secretary Bob Finch, was there too, with his wife. We had drinks before dinner, which I was glad for. I'd just picked up a cocktail when the president pulled me aside.

"Let's talk for a minute," he said.

I took a deep breath to calm myself as we moved to a quiet corner. Nixon, who'd had a couple cocktails himself, seemed quite relaxed. He put a hand on my shoulder and gave me a fatherly pat.

"Bob, I know how you feel about that article. They've done the same damn thing to me. Don't let it get to you, and don't worry about it. I want you to know that I think you are doing a great job. I want you to stay at the White House and just keep doing what you've been doing. You have my full support, and if anybody tries to block you in your efforts, you can come to me."

I appreciated his gesture and his support. It was time to tune out the critics and focus on proving them wrong.

IN HIS INAUGURAL ADDRESS on January 20, 1969, Nixon emphasized a theme we'd first seen on a banner at a campaign stop in Deshler, Ohio. A thirteen-year-old girl named Vicki Cole had held up a sign saying BRING US TOGETHER, and Nixon picked up on that message.

Following that theme, I had suggested that Nixon reach out to blacks in his speech, and he did. "No man can be fully free while his neighbor is not. To go forward at all is to go forward together. This means black and white together, as one nation, not two."

Despite his pledge, there were not many believers among the protestors lined up along Pennsylvania Avenue to confront the new president after the ceremony. They chanted antiwar slogans and held up posters denouncing Nixon as a war criminal. Some burned the little American flags that had been handed out by Boy Scouts. When the motorcade approached the area of 13th and 14th Streets, protestors threw sticks, stones, beer cans, and smoke bombs at the president's limousine.

Most new presidents enjoy a honeymoon period with the press and the public as they settle into office and familiarize themselves with the issues. Nixon didn't have much of a honeymoon, and neither did those of us on his staff. Rapidly escalating antiwar sentiments and the volatile issue of school desegregation had the nation in a state of high anxiety. Fourteen years after the Supreme Court declared that segregated schools were unconstitutional, very little, if anything, had been done to remedy the situation. Only 5 percent of black schoolchildren in the South attended desegregated schools.

One presidential administration after another had ducked the issue. Nobody really wanted to be associated with forcibly busing schoolchildren to meet the Supreme Court's demands. Yet something had to be done.

Just nine days into Nixon's first term, his administration came under heavy fire for refusing to cut federal aid to five segregated Southern school districts that had not met the deadline for devising court-ordered desegregation plans. Instead they were given a sixty-day extension. Many black leaders took it as a sure sign that Nixon was going to turn the clock back on civil rights and desegregation.

But that wasn't the plan at all. Nixon publicly stated that the *Brown* decision was correct "in both constitutional and human terms," and he declared his intention to enforce the law. From the very start, the president had asked us to find a way to bring about desegregation in the South without violence. Under the leadership of Secretary of Labor George P. Shultz, we'd quietly been putting together a strategy to achieve that. My High Point friend Dr. Tom Haggai, a former pastor who became president of IGA supermarkets, traveled the Southern states with me to convince business and community leaders that peaceful desegregation was vital for the good of our nation.

Nixon met personally in the White House with many of those leaders from across the South. He would begin each meeting in a calm manner, asking for cooperation and assistance, but he always concluded by sternly noting that anyone who stirred up resistance to desegregation would face "a pox on your house."

President Nixon rarely gets the credit he deserves for this, but he effectively brought about a peaceful desegregation of schools in the South. He always assured me that he was determined to have a real impact on the lives of black Americans, but one of the first things he did was more of a symbolic gesture, not to mention a whole lot of fun. It was a grand party for Duke Ellington at the White House on April 29, 1969. Nixon presented the famed musician and bandleader with the ultimate birthday gift: the Presidential Medal of Freedom.

I wish I could say this party was my idea, but it was his legal and domestic affairs advisor, Len Garment, who suggested it. Garment was a jazz saxophonist who played with Woody Herman's band before earning a law degree and heading to a career on Wall Street.

Some reports later called the party "the biggest Negro event in the history of the White House." It certainly was a night that Sallie and I would never forget. All of the racial and social unrest was put aside for one evening, and everyone cut loose. Nixon was more animated than I'd ever seen him. He never stopped smiling and laughing.

Sallie and I talked, laughed, and danced until we dropped. In one of our most memorable moments, the Duke walked up to us with a much younger woman on his arm. Sallie had enjoyed a couple cocktails by then, so she sidled up to the guest of honor and asked how he was doing. Then she said, "And who is this young lady?"

Duke smiled slyly and said, "She Jane, me Tarzan."

I laughed so hard I thought I was going to fall down. Sallie was not quite as amused.

Someone later said this rollicking party was like the White House had swallowed up the Cotton Club. The music was incredible. Cab Calloway, Mahalia Jackson, Dizzy Gillespie, Billy Eckstine, Lou Rawls, Benny Goodman, Earl Hines, Marian McPartland, and Dave Brubeck traded licks with the Duke and an all-star band all night long. They were even jamming with the U.S. Marine Band, not to mention a strolling accordion player.

Even Vice President Agnew got in the act. He chased a Marine pianist off his bench and played a Greek politician's interpretation of his favorite Ellington tunes, "In a Sentimental Mood" and "Sophisticated Lady."

Not to be outdone, the commander in chief took command of the keys on the White House Steinway grand, ordered the assembled dignitaries to prepare for the key of G, and led us all in singing "Happy Birthday" to the guest of honor.

The music stopped only long enough for the president to present the Medal of Freedom to his guest. "In the royalty of American music, no man swings more or stands higher than the Duke," he said.

The night was particularly memorable for the Duke because his father had once worked as a butler in the White House. He proclaimed he hadn't been that happy since he'd been a baby in his mother's arms. The Duke was so happy, in fact, that he announced his intention to kiss everybody at the party on both cheeks, and he did—women, men, and the president himself.

THE PARTY WENT until 2:30 a.m., but the last notes from the Duke's band had hardly faded when the Reverend Ralph Abernathy came calling for a showdown with the president, and I got caught in the crossfire. The SCLC president didn't have any faith that Nixon would take an interest in supporting racial equality. He'd started attacking the Nixon administration before Inauguration Day, and he didn't let up.

I was surprised then, in May of that year, when I learned that Ralph and an entourage were planning a major conference on poverty and minority issues with the president, members of Patrick Moynihan's newly formed Urban Affairs Council, and various Cabinet and staff members.

I was even more displeased to learn I'd been purposely excluded from planning sessions for that meeting. I was told that Abernathy had asked that Moynihan, not me, serve as their liaison for the meeting with the president. I was hurt by that. I'd worked alongside Ralph for years at the SCLC. I'd also stepped up and helped raise money and bring in supplies for the Poor People's Campaign, which was staged under Ralph's leadership.

I would not have been so upset at being excluded from the planning for this meeting if I'd been told directly by Ralph or another SCLC senior staffer. Instead, I learned about it through other channels.

I didn't complain. I had a thousand other things going on. Still, I thought they'd made a mistake. Moynihan certainly did not have the history with the SCLC that I had, and he would have his hands full if this meeting went the way I expected. Ralph's primary agenda would be to make himself look like a tough leader who was unafraid to confront the president of the United States.

The meeting was scheduled for the Roosevelt Room. As soon as Ralph showed up at the White House security gate, I received a call to go down and deal with the fact that he'd brought more than thirty people with him. The president intensely disliked meeting with large groups, and this was a potentially hostile affair.

I was ordered to cull the crowd. I supported the SCLC and the purpose of the meeting, but I had no qualms about following the directive. I went down and told Ralph that he would have to choose a more reasonable number of representatives, and the rest of the people would have to wait elsewhere.

After protesting mildly, he made his selections. I then asked security to escort the remaining two dozen members of his entourage off the White House grounds. I told the Secret Service team to take them across the narrow alley to the Executive Office Building, where I worked. They were taken to the ornate and historic Indian Treaty Room on the top floor, where they soon opened the windows and began to hoot and holler, acting like unruly football fans whose team was being thrashed on the field.

I then escorted Rev. Abernathy, Rev. Lowery, and the others into the Roosevelt Room. If I had been asked to help with the meeting's planning, I would have coached Ralph to engage Nixon in conversation rather than dictating to him. The president enjoyed intelligent one-on-one give-and-take, even if his policies were being questioned.

Instead, Ralph began their meeting with a nine-page statement apparently intended to echo Dr. King's "I Have a Dream" speech. It was a poor imitation. "I am concerned . . ." was Ralph's repeated phrase. He then enumerated a wide-ranging list of his concerns, from the war in Vietnam to ABM missiles and rising unemployment.

Nixon tried to reach out. He expressed his determination to

end American involvement in Vietnam without danger of being drawn back in. The president noted that he and many of his staff members had grown up in poverty, and so were aware of the issues and were committed to addressing them.

At first, Ralph seemed to grasp that Nixon wasn't unsympathetic, but as the meeting progressed, he grew more and more sullen. Initially, he seemed to indicate that he would support Nixon's presidency. Later, he curtly demanded to have individual meetings with certain Cabinet members. Nixon gestured around the room at all of those assembled and told Ralph to "have at 'em."

The president then left. He'd had enough. The meeting went on for nearly three more hours, with Moynihan refereeing and taking notes. I was embarrassed for my former civil rights comrades. What happened in that meeting was symptomatic of the struggling civil rights movement. It had become fragmented, unfocused, and self-defeating. Some of the comments and allegations bordered on paranoia.

A Native American woman in the group claimed that there was a government plan to exterminate her tribe. A black woman said that Nixon wanted blacks to return to Africa, and that the government had lied about the moon landings. She then said her people were going to "destroy you" if God didn't.

The embarrassment did not end there.

When the meeting ended, Moynihan, press secretary Ron Ziegler, and I were among those who accompanied the Reverend Ralph Abernathy and the Reverend Joe Lowery, another civil rights warrior I'd known for many years, to the front entrance of the West Wing. Television and print reporters were gathered there to interview them about the meeting.

My impression was that Nixon had been receptive and open to more communication with Abernathy—and he certainly hadn't been dismissive. But when the camera lights came on, Ralph put an entirely different spin on it. He spoke in angry bursts: "It was the most fruitless and the most disappointing of all the meetings we have had up to this time," he claimed.

I was stunned. Moynihan and Ziegler shot death-ray looks at me. I felt sick. Then Moynihan turned to me and said, "Goddamn it, Bob, your people just pissed all over the president."

He was throwing me under the bus for a disastrous meeting that he'd controlled from the beginning. I ripped into him for that, and he was lucky I didn't do more. Ron Ziegler all but pushed us into his office to keep our heated conversation private.

"We don't have time for this," Ziegler said. "We need to work this out."

In the meantime, the rowdies I'd sent to the Indian Treaty Room were hanging out windows and yelling insults at the president and his staff while cheering on Rev. Abernathy.

"Give 'em hell, Ralph!"

"You tell those damn crackers, Reverend!"

"Nixon hates blacks!"

News cameras and reporters caught it all. I was appalled and embarrassed. I had dared hope this meeting might establish some lines of communication between civil rights groups and the White House. But the longest meeting ever between black leaders and an American president had turned into a fiasco.

If our administration was going to make any progress in elevating the lives of those who needed it most, we would have to do it another way.

Chapter 11

WORKING WITHIN THE SYSTEM

FOR A WHILE, RALPH ABERNATHY'S PUBLIC LAMBASTING OF Nixon made my life miserable. CBS anchorman Walter Cronkite noted in his evening report that Abernathy's tirade was "the strongest dressing-down of any president on his own doorstep in the memory of veteran White House correspondents."

I don't think Ralph did his cause any good in ticking off Nixon. After seeing the press reports on the backlash, the president wrote a note to Haldeman and John Ehrlichman, Nixon's assistant for domestic affairs, that said, "This shows that my judgment about not seeing such people is right. No more of this!"

I apologized to the president on behalf of "such people" everywhere, and then went back to trying to accomplish my mission from the inside, despite all the sabotage from friends on the outside.

On the day of Rev. Abernathy's contentious meeting with the president and his Cabinet, there sat on my office desk an inch-thick *Catalog of Federal Assistance for Minority Entrepreneurs*. It was a groundwork document compiled as part of our plan to deliver federal funds directly to minority men and women so that they could become owners instead of renters, CEOs instead of employees, and full participants in building the American economy.

Blacks then comprised about 11 percent of the country's population, but we owned less than 5 percent of the nation's businesses and a paltry 1 percent of its business assets. I knew firsthand why so many blacks struggled to start businesses and keep them running. It was all but impossible for most to get bank financing for a startup.

We didn't need handouts; we needed access to capital.

In the first few weeks of Nixon's administration, we put together a committee on minority enterprise to come up with ways to spur black capitalism. My research found that the Democrats had created more than one hundred programs to encourage black economic development, but most of them were inactive. Very few people had used them or benefited from them. President Nixon wanted better results.

"Now I know all the words. I know all the gimmicks and the phrases that would win the applause of black audiences and professional civil rights leaders. I am not going to use them. I am interested in deeds," he said in February of 1970.

Our mission was to establish an umbrella organization to pull together the best of those scattered and ineffective minority programs—and their funds—and reactivate them. That's what we did. The new entity didn't need funding. The money was already allocated for the individual programs. There were millions available that had been untapped.

On March 15, 1969, President Nixon signed an executive order establishing the Office of Minority Business Enterprise (OMBE) within the Department of Commerce. This was an ambitious, multiphase attack on discrimination, segregation, and racism. At the same time, the president also signed an executive order empowering the Commerce Department to coordinate other federal programs supporting minority business development.

This marked the first time a U.S. president had issued an executive order spelling out the government's responsibility to involve blacks in the free enterprise system. Basically, we were creating a government-funded business incubator and venture capital fund to enable blacks and other minorities to start their own businesses, and to share in government contracting opportunities. This was a game changer that would have a lasting, positive impact. And it was long overdue, because too many had been denied access to the American Dream for too long.

Members of our committee traveled the country, drumming up support for the black entrepreneurship program. We visited top executives at Ford, McDonald's, and other major companies, pushing them to promote blacks, develop training and franchise programs for them, and otherwise do whatever they could to reach out and bring more minorities into the economy.

We not only preached the gospel, we did what we could to carry it out. One of our creations in the Small Business Administration encouraged large corporations to give loans to minority small-business owners by lending them two dollars for every one dollar they invested with a minority business. By the mid-1970s, corporations such as General Motors, Rockwell International, Sears, and other Fortune 500 companies were helping support more than eighty of these black-owned businesses with $40 million in capital.

This was the sort of economic empowerment for black Americans that the Reverend Martin Luther King Jr. had been pushing for before his death. We were working the system for the greater good of all people.

LATE IN OUR first year in the White House, I wrote a memo encouraging all federal agencies to establish their own goals for expanding purchase programs with minority firms. The president signed my memo and gave me his full support. Even Pat Moynihan publicly praised it as "the most powerful engine" ever established to promote minority business development.

Up to that point, black, Hispanic, and other minority-owned companies were generally cut out of the bidding process for government contracts, which seriously crippled their ability to grow beyond a few full-time employees. We began putting money in places that would have a real impact on the lives of blacks and other minorities. We went about this in a relatively quiet way because we didn't want to raise expectations, we wanted to elevate lives.

We also devised the "set-aside" program in which government agencies were required to reserve a portion of all of their contracts for minority-owned businesses granted special status. These approved minority-owned companies could be awarded federal contracts without having to bid against larger competitors, but only if the contracts were less than $5 million for manufacturing and $3 million for other services.

We were getting things done, but it wasn't always easy. I quickly learned that I had to protect myself and my position from those who failed to recognize my responsibilities. One day early on in my White House tenure, I learned that another aide, Len Garment, had set up a preliminary meeting with several black members of Congress who wanted to arrange a conference with the president.

I didn't even hear about Garment's meeting until I was on my way out of town on a trip. I sent one of my aides to it, and he came back with a list of things that they'd decided *I* should do to help them prepare for the meeting with the president.

They hadn't invited me to the meeting, but they'd thrown a bunch of work at me. I put the word out that I was preparing to resign because of efforts to marginalize me.

Within a few hours, Nixon asked to meet with me. I walked into the Oval Office and Nixon greeted me warmly. John Ehrlichman was sitting off to the side—a fly on the wall that I hadn't expected.

Nixon tried to calm me down. "Bob, you know I like you very much and I don't want you to quit."

Ehrlichman seemed preoccupied. He was taking notes on a yellow legal pad. The president turned to him and said, "John, I don't want this to happen to Bob anymore."

Ehrlichman continued taking notes and didn't look up.

Nixon snapped at him: "Goddamn it, John, listen to me. I want

Bob all the way in or all the way out. And I don't want this to happen again."

That got Ehrlichman's attention.

"Yes sir, Bob will have everything he needs from now on," he said.

From that time on, I was informed of every meeting in the White House that touched on my areas of responsibility. These included minority and racial affairs as well as emergency and disaster management, but my primary focus was always on black economic development. My goal was to attack poverty and racial discrimination by creating opportunities for financial independence.

After my meeting with Nixon and Ehrlichman, I was even invited to all Cabinet meetings, which was rare for someone in my position. In fact, they invited me to more meetings than I could possibly attend. Still, that was the way I wanted it. If I had to pound the table and slam some doors to make that clear, I was willing to do it.

WITHIN A FEW MONTHS of Nixon's inauguration, we'd launched so many initiatives and pilot programs that even the nationally syndicated columnist Carl Rowan had to give us a tip of the hat: "For where Mr. Nixon is entitled to the applause of the black community, he ought to get it."

It was all about building black power from within the system, and make no mistake, there were many of us quietly working the civil rights agenda from within the system. Arthur Fletcher ranks right at the top of those pushing for change from the inside. Arthur was a very charismatic, savvy guy who'd played in the NFL in the 1950s, but he made an even bigger mark as the father of modern affirmative action programs. His stroke of genius was a new version of the "Philadelphia Plan," which said that if you were working on government contracts, you had to hire a certain percentage of blacks. We faced a lot of resistance even from within the federal government, and were subjected to personal attacks as well, but we pushed it through and millions of minorities benefited.

It's impossible to measure the full impact of the OMBE and all of its programs. I am certain, however, that it had a great deal of responsibility for the unprecedented rise in black-owned businesses in this country, not to mention the increasing number of minorities who ranked in the upper ranges of income.

We took a lot of flak from Democrats and other skeptics who claimed Nixon didn't care about black America. Still, even some die-hard Democrats knew that blacks inside the Nixon administration were quietly pushing the agenda endorsed by Dr. King. One of those in the know was my old friend Earl G. Graves, who was a leading black Democrat at the forefront of pushing for black entrepreneurship and economic growth. He saw that with the OMBE, Nixon was reaching out with a program unlike any others.

This was also a personal issue for Earl. In August of 1970, he launched his own nonprofit Black Enterprise institute. Its goals were much the same as mine. Earl had long wanted to create a magazine to champion black business development and wealth-building in the black community, but he had not been able to raise the capital. He was about $100,000 short of his goal.

I encouraged him to apply for one of the first OMBE grants. When word got out that Earl Graves, a big Democrat and a frequent critic of Nixon, had applied for the grant, there was heated opposition from partisan Republican operatives who didn't want it approved. I argued forcefully that Earl wanted the same things we wanted for black America, and that if we helped him develop his business, he would support economic development in the black community.

They told me I was nuts, not to mention naive and probably numb-skulled too. My final response was: "Process his damn application!"

Commerce secretary Maurice Stans had to sign off on these loans and grants. He called and told me he was getting a lot of flak about the Earl Graves application. I told him Earl was a former Green Beret officer and federal narcotics agent, as well as a patriot and a champion of black economic development whom I could personally vouch for.

Stans signed the papers and Earl got his money. His *Black Enterprise* magazine quickly became a cheerleader for black economic empowerment. And the grant didn't keep Earl from expressing his Democratic Party principles. He let fire whenever he thought the Republicans weren't doing the right thing. He stayed true to his party and to his beliefs. Yet he also gave Nixon credit when credit was due. That was all we asked.

In 1981, *Black Enterprise* reported that 56 of the top 100 black businesses in the country were started between 1969 and 1976. Thirty of them were created between 1969 and 1971 when the Office of Minority Business Enterprise was kicking into gear.

The most gratifying experience of my tenure in the White House was seeing minority-owned businesses all over the country benefit from this program. This was the reason I'd accepted the job with Nixon, and the reason I gave up my own business and spent so much time away from Sallie, the love of my life. We leveled the playing field for those who had been held back by racial discrimination, Jim Crow laws, and slavery before that. We were wielding the power of the federal government to enact long-term social change.

INCREASING ECONOMIC opportunities for minorities was my primary focus for the Nixon administration, but it wasn't *all* I had on my plate. It seemed like I'd been working for the president only five or ten minutes when the first president of a black college came to me asking for assistance.

They'd been pounding on the door of the White House for years, and finally they found someone who'd let them in. For some reason, black schools of higher education had been cut out of the flow of federal dollars that most public colleges and universities received. Millions had been set aside for black colleges by an act of Congress in 1965, but the money had never been released.

I learned that someone had written into the legislation a phrase that effectively cut off their funding, and only theirs. This phrase said any school receiving these federal funds had to come up with a matching amount of money in order to qualify. Historically black colleges simply did not have the fund-raising capabilities of other schools, which was the reason they needed federal money in the first place. Nixon had once told me, "I want you to decide what needs to be fixed and fix it." This was definitely something that needed a major repair job.

When I told him about this issue, Nixon allowed me to round up $100 million in grants for black colleges and universities. Still, the federal agencies that controlled those funds fought me, claiming there was no way to do it without new legislation or an act of God.

Instead of God, I found Emery Bacon. Or actually, Emery found me. He was executive director of an obscure committee on education, but he wasn't your typical bureaucrat. He'd been a Fulbright scholar. He'd attended Oxford University and the University of Pittsburgh law school after earning advanced degrees in Latin and Greek.

Emery called me one day and claimed he'd come up with a "relatively easy" solution. We met and I liked him immediately. He had a strong sense of justice. He also knew how to play the game. He circumvented the partisan political process and the red tape of government bureaucracy by drafting a provision that allowed federal funds to flow to any college or university that served students primarily from poverty-level families. That resulted in millions and millions of dollars being released to every predominantly black college and university in the country.

We pushed it through and the impact was dramatic. From 1970 to 1971, federal aid to black colleges and universities increased 16 percent over the previous year—by $125 million. Two years later, the amount doubled to $200 million.

Officials at the long-neglected black schools were ecstatic. And today, I have so many honorary degrees from black and white schools that I've run out of places to hang them. I have boxes of those plaques still around the house. Every time I see them, or trip over them, or have to move them, I'm reminded of the parable of the loaves and the fishes, one of my grandmother's favorites.

Mama always contributed a few dollars to the Sunday church collection, even though she had no money to spare. As a child with holes in his shoes, I wasn't inclined to be so generous. She'd give me a few coins to put in the basket and I'd palm at least a nickel or two so I could buy candy later. One Sunday, she caught me in the act. I argued that a nickel or two wouldn't make much difference in the collection. She countered that whatever we gave, God would multiply, just as Jesus had with the loaves and the fishes.

"Bobby, you should give whatever you've got, because you can't out-give God," she said. "He won't let you."

Chapter 12

SOMETHING BIGGER THAN YOU

Along with my other duties, I served as president Nixon's designated troubleshooter for black America, bringing aid to communities that had been hit by disasters—natural or man-made. I relished this role, which, as far as I can tell, was unique and unprecedented in the history of presidential administrations.

I was thirty-three years old, energetic, and eager to serve. Honestly, sometimes I felt like a superhero flying to the rescue, helping people in need, doing good things for communities that had been neglected or struck by disaster. Imagine how heady it was to order up a plane from the White House, load it with top-ranking officials from every relevant government agency needed, and then fly into areas desperate for assistance. It was beyond anything you could dream to walk off that big ol' plane with the full power of the federal government at my disposal and say, "What can we do to help?" And it was especially gratifying when we proved our critics wrong.

NAACP president Roy Wilkins asked for a meeting with President Nixon in January of 1969. He said he had several matters on his agenda, but most pressing was the need for a stronger federal response to twin disasters that had struck in southern Mississippi just a week or so before. He complained that the response had been inadequate, and perhaps racially motivated, because the hardest-hit areas were poor black enclaves.

The first disaster had been a massive tornado that tore through six counties, killing 32 people and injuring 241. The second blow came two days later when a Southern Railway freight train with 139 cars derailed while passing through the small town of Laurel in the same region.

Fourteen tanker cars of propane gas exploded in the downtown area. News reports said two people were killed, thirty-three were hospitalized, and more than 1,350 homes were damaged in a city already hard-hit by the tornado. Laurel, an old cotton mill and manufacturing town, had been a hotbed of KKK activity and racial division during the civil rights years. Its impoverished black neighborhoods and communities were all but destroyed by the two calamities.

It irked me that Roy Wilkins hadn't called me when he wanted help for those people in Mississippi. We knew each other well. He knew I was on Nixon's staff. Apparently he didn't think I had the power to help him.

President Nixon set him straight. When Roy Wilkins walked into the Oval Office and said we needed to mount federal resources to help those hit by the two disasters, the president said:

"Bob here handles a lot of things for me, and he should be your contact person in the future. We want to be helpful any way we can. I'd like to have a good relationship with you and the NAACP."

Roy still seemed skeptical, but when he outlined some specifics for what was needed in Mississippi, the president made a few notes and then turned to me.

"Bob, get right on that and do whatever is necessary to take care of it."

"I'll be on a plane in the morning," I said.

That seemed to please Wilkins, who then moved on to his "other matters." He asked the president to intercede on behalf of a friend in the Department of Labor who was in danger of losing his job.

Nixon listened and again turned to me:

"Bob, will you handle that?"

"Yes sir, I'll get right on it," I said.

Wilkins next asked the president to consider another of his friends for a federal judgeship.

"See to that, will you, Bob?" Nixon said.

"Yes sir," I said.

Roy Wilkins was put on notice after that, and I did everything I could to prove to him and the rest of the country that I was trustworthy, and that I could get things done. Every day the calls came to my office from old church friends, contacts from my civil rights days, or just people in impoverished and neglected communities who'd heard that I was willing to listen.

I soon found myself flying all over the country, heading up task forces to assist those in need. It was shocking how many black towns lacked not only paved roads but water systems and sewage treatment plants.

I opened up the federal coffers to them all. I'd fly in with a planeload of top administrators from every federal agency needed to help. We made a real difference in impoverished black towns like Roosevelt City, Alabama, where we set up federal funding for a city hall, a new jail, and a community center while also providing surplus emergency vehicles for their police and fire departments.

Perhaps my most challenging troubleshooting assignment came in 1970, when President Nixon heard reports of racism and racial conflicts on U.S. military bases around the world. He put me in charge of a task force and I spent a couple of years traveling to bases around the world, investigating racism and recommending changes.

Racial unrest was still a problem throughout the country. Some argued that the military's problems reflected what was happening everywhere. There were full-scale race riots in almost every major U.S. city and many smaller towns from 1969 to 1972. Those tensions had spread to military bases, ships, and even Coast Guard stations in the United States, Vietnam, and Germany.

Our task force found that racism ran from the top down in all branches of our armed services. It was destroying military discipline and unity in every corner of the world. We'd even had persistent reports of Ku Klux Klan cells operating on military bases in Germany.

Military brass went into full denial mode. In one case, I flew to Keesler Air Force Base in Biloxi, Mississippi, and met with the base commander, who said he had racial matters under control. I had a stack of letters that said otherwise. I informed him that I'd be touring not just the base, but also the local entertainment district just outside the gates.

We went with a caravan of officers and a military police escort. We'd been driving only a few minutes when it became obvious that our escorts were trying to steer us away from certain restaurants and bars near the base. My information said these were the places where blacks were denied access.

I ordered my driver to take a detour. We pulled into a parking lot where I'd seen white soldiers leaving a restaurant. There were many soldiers coming and going; none of them looked anything like me. I opened my car door and got out.

The colonel accompanying us tried to head me off.

"These are just local dives," he said.

"Well then, I think I'll dive right in," I replied.

I'd just walked in the door when a woman in a white blouse with her hair up in a bun hustled over. I thought she might want to take my drink order, but instead she gave me an order of her own.

"You can't come in here. We don't allow no coloreds."

"But we are military men and I see all of these soldiers in here," I said.

"They are all white, you see, we don't allow colored."

The colonel did a poor job of pretending to be surprised at this.

I instructed the base commander to ban *all* service personnel from entering any whites-only restaurants, clubs, or shops in the community. The town around the base was fully integrated within forty-eight hours.

RARELY WERE RACIAL problems in the military so easily resolved. My investigation also found that there were very few or no black officers at the top-rank levels in any of the armed services, which gave the rank and file nowhere to turn when they encountered racism. Nixon told me to order up promotions of qualified black officers. He mentioned one name in particular, a war hero by the name of Daniel "Chappie" James Jr.

Chappie was an Air Force fighter pilot who had trained as a Tuskegee airman in World War II and flown more than 175 combat missions in Korea and Vietnam. Under Nixon's orders, he'd been promoted to one-star brigadier general and assigned to the Pentagon, where he served as deputy assistant secretary for public affairs in the Department of Defense.

Chappie and I became good friends. He wanted to become the first black four-star general, and he'd certainly earned that rank, but he'd been passed over several times and he was discouraged. I talked to both Haldeman and Ehrlichman. They agreed that General James was a deserving candidate. The president agreed. Nixon said he would refuse to sign any promotion list that didn't have Chappie's or any other minority name on it.

When the Pentagon's next promotion list came to the White House, Haldeman had me review it. There weren't any blacks on the list at all. We sent it back without the president's signature.

The Pentagon sent a new list. There were no blacks on that list either, so back it went.

This went on for months. Finally the Pentagon sent over a list that had Chappie's promotion and those of two or three other well-deserving black officers.

The president approved them all.

Chappie became the first black officer in the history of the United States military to be awarded four stars. His first post was commander of the North American Air Defense Command (NORAD).

I still get emotional when I think about his long but ultimately successful fight. Chappie died in 1978, just one month after his retirement. I admired him greatly. Like many blacks in the military, he had to fight for the recognition he'd earned throughout a distinguished career serving his country. During Nixon's first term, the number of black generals and admirals increased from two to fourteen. His administration appointed the first black assistant secretary of the Navy, and the first black to serve on the U.S. Court of Appeals for the Armed Forces.

Not everyone was a fan of these efforts. General William C. Westmoreland, the U.S. Army's chief of staff, was among those who complained about my "meddling" in military promotions. The army had more racial problems than any other division, but they refused to send representatives to my meetings. I put out word that if there wasn't more cooperation, top brass could kiss their stars and their careers goodbye. I even threatened to call out Nixon's notorious pit-bull twins, Ehrlichman and Haldeman.

A short time later, John Ehrlichman informed me that General Westmoreland had requested a meeting with the president.

"I told him to come on over," Ehrlichman said. "But he won't be seeing the old man."

Instead, the general walked into Ehrlichman's office and found John and Yours Truly waiting for him. Westmoreland's face turned a deep crimson when he saw me there.

At that moment, the general realized he'd been messing with the wrong guy.

Ehrlichman asked Westmoreland what his complaints were.

"Mr. Brown is sending too many orders. We have a job to do and we are trying to carry out our mission . . ."

When Westmoreland finished his spiel, Ehrlichman looked at me and gave me the command to fire at will: "Bob, what do you have to say?"

I opened a folder and spread on the conference table reports of racial riots and racial violence in our army posts around the world. I told him that the army's failure to deal with these problems was threatening our national security, not to mention the reputation of our commander in chief.

Ehrlichman then explained to General Westmoreland that I was following Nixon's orders to clean up this problem, and that the army had better cooperate with me.

Westmoreland was furious, but like a good soldier, he controlled his anger.

"I will do as you have ordered," he said. "And I have no problem working with Mr. Brown."

I wasn't completely buying it. Even as he spoke those words, the general seemed defiant, clenching his jaw and glaring at me across the conference table. I could see Ehrlichman taking it all in, maybe even enjoying the confrontation.

My anger rose as I thought of all the reports I'd read of blacks being discriminated against, denied promotions, given the most dangerous assignments, and handed much worse punishments than whites for the same military crimes.

I went a little mad-dog, telling the general in no uncertain terms that he would either cooperate with me or I'd move him the hell out of my way.

"General, I'm here to get a job done and I want it done now. Not on your time or the army's time, but on the president's timetable. When I call a meeting, I want your team there, and I want the information I request from them to be delivered to me on schedule. Are we clear on that?"

Westmoreland said he would see to it that my wishes were followed. Ehrlichman drove his point home one more time:

"General, are we all clear on this?"

"I'm very clear," Westmoreland said.

From that point on, I had no more problems with General Westmoreland. If I wanted three of his staff people for a meeting, they were there. If I wanted to visit a military base anywhere in the world, I was offered total access and given full support. As a result, we made sweeping changes in the way blacks were treated in the U.S. armed services.

I still hear from members of that first generation of black military leaders who were promoted under my watch. Sometimes their sons and daughters send me letters to share their appreciation and memories of what those worthy men told them about their long, hard fight for the ranks they deserved.

I was burning with ambition and drive back in those White House years. My anger over injustice drove me, as did my faith and the belief implanted in me from childhood. That voice that said, *Never forget, child, that you were put on this Earth to do something bigger than you.*

Chapter 13

THE LORD WILL TAKE CARE OF THE REST

IN THE LATE 1960S, A BLACK MAN SPIT ON ME AS I WAS WALK-
ing through the lobby of the Barringer Hotel in Charlotte,
North Carolina. He shouted that I had sold out and betrayed my
own people because I worked for Richard Nixon.

I don't recall any other details, and I'm mostly glad for that flaw
in my otherwise strong memory. To dwell on moments like that
would have been my undoing. Too much anger was attached to
those memories. You can't contain those powerful feelings. Rage
will destroy you from the inside out.

Still, for every award that came my way during my years with
Nixon, there were three or four rebukes, criticisms, or attacks. A
Washington reporter who caught me in an unguarded moment
early in my White House years asked me about all the criticism and
threats I received for joining the Nixon administration. His story
quoted me saying that I still carried a knife and knew how to use it.

I came upon that newspaper clipping while doing research for
this book, and it startled me to see how close to the surface my
anger remained. Many times, I wanted to lash out. I had to try to
shed that part of myself to function in the public eye.

Most black men and women who achieve any level of success go
through the same thing. They are questioned and criticized and
distrusted from all sides. From the inside, too. *Why did I make it?
Why me? Did I betray something to get here?*

Whenever I felt the rage rising, I'd purposefully envision my grandmother, the daughter of a slave, working as a cleaning lady for the white folks. Mama handled her life with such courage and strength. She once had a neighbor lady try to poison her for some demented reason. Mama prayed for her and overpowered her with kindness.

Her strength humbled me, and her words put me back on course. "You can't go wrong doing right. So, keep doing good and the Lord will take care of the rest." I was in a unique position to make a difference in the lives of those who'd been ignored and forgotten.

"You can't do evil for evil. You have to fight it," Mama would say. "Fight evil with good."

It was never, ever easy to do it her way.

"If you can't forget it, then you haven't forgiven," she'd say. But some things weren't so easy to forget.

THE GREATEST SOURCE of black hostility toward Richard Nixon was the perception that he was not committed to school desegregation. Nixon believed that no black student should be denied the right to attend any public school, but like many people, black and white, he had strong misgivings about the forced busing of children to accomplish a social goal. Very few people really thought busing was a great solution, especially if it was their own kids or grandkids being bused to distant schools.

A 1971 poll by George Gallup found that 76 percent of Americans opposed busing to achieve racial balance. Gallup wrote that the overwhelming disapproval of busing was "political dynamite" that strengthened Nixon's position of opposing it. The same poll found that in the South, 82 percent of voters, black and white, opposed busing.

Nixon believed that the Supreme Court was right in ordering

all schools to be desegregated. He just thought it was wrong to force a child to travel fifteen miles on a bus simply to achieve racial balance.

It is also true, of course, that Nixon did not want to commit political suicide by alienating more conservative voters—his primary supporters—with forced busing. He wanted to end busing quietly, without bloodshed, and without cutting his throat with conservative whites.

Nixon didn't commit publicly to either side, but he told us to get the job done. And we did. We put together what today might be called a "stealth" desegregation plan for the South. We tried to convince state and community leaders that peaceful desegregation was in their best interests. If we had to, we twisted their arms by reminding them that their access to federal contracts, grants, and assistance depended on their cooperation.

We integrated public schools in the South, for the most part avoiding open confrontation. Prior to 1969, only 186,000 out of three million black students were in desegregated schools. By the fall of that year, 600,000 black school kids sat in desegregated Southern classrooms, and a year later the number had grown to two million.

We didn't get much credit for pulling it off at the time, because Nixon's critics focused on his refusal to force busing or to cut off federal funds to school districts that didn't comply with court-ordered desegregation plans.

IN JANUARY OF 1972, several of my Washington friends told me they wanted to have a dinner for me, but they described it mostly as a benefit for foster care children in DC, sickle cell anemia research, and causes like the United Negro College Fund.

They were being sneaky. I later found out they'd secretly planned the benefit to give me a boost because I'd been taking so much heat in the press and from black Democrats. Whatever their motives, this was the evening of a lifetime for me and those I loved.

More than three thousand people came to the event at the Washington Hilton and Towers. Guests included members of Congress and the Supreme Court, White House staffers, civil rights leaders, educators, business leaders, entertainers, and athletes. Supreme Court justice William H. Rehnquist was there, along with the Apollo 17 astronauts, the first black to play major league baseball, Jackie Robinson, and the Godfather of Soul, James Brown, who had supported Nixon and his anti-drug program.

I was honored that so many celebrated people came, and even more flattered when I learned that a group of civic and business leaders from my hometown had chartered a plane so that they could come too. I didn't think about it until much later, but I had once caddied for many of the white hometown executives who flew in for my benefit. A local leader and friend, attorney J. V. Morgan, led this effort.

The headliner was entertainer Sammy Davis Jr., which was fitting because Sammy, too, had taken considerable flak for supporting Nixon. I felt bad for him, because Sammy was a man of generous spirit who had donated and raised millions for the civil rights movement. I had talked him into serving on Nixon's advisory board to the Council of Economic Opportunity. When he flew in for their quarterly meetings, Sammy always stopped by my office. Sallie and I became good friends with the entertainer and his wife, Altovise.

Sammy understood my position all too well. In his autobiography, *Why Me?*, Sammy wrote, "With all of John Kennedy's liberalism, never did he have a black man anywhere near as close to him as Robert Brown was to Richard Nixon."

Sammy himself grew close enough to Nixon to correct the president during one visit. They had a private chat, and afterward Sammy came into my office laughing hysterically. Nixon had used the term "Negro," and Sammy, ever the hipster, told him that it was no longer cool.

"We say 'black' now," Sammy had told the commander in chief.

"How did that happen?" Nixon replied.

Sammy may have been the main entertainment at the party, but my most special guest was my grandmother, Miss Nellie Brown. I choke up just thinking about Mama being there that night. Before the party, Sallie took her shopping in Washington and she bought this beautiful, very fashionable floral print dress. She also wore her favorite Sunday hat, which I still have at home as a keepsake.

My grandmother sat with me at the head table, and I can attest to the fact that she had the time of her life. She loved the limelight, and everyone fawned over her. Such a joy it was to see her, the daughter of a slave, raised in a big shack in eastern North Carolina with nine sisters and one brother, talking and laughing with senators and Supreme Court justices.

She looked absolutely regal, sipping her coffee—she loved coffee—and taking it all in.

President Nixon had told me earlier that he couldn't make the honorary event because of a previous commitment, but he'd sent a very nice letter of congratulations. I was grateful, of course, but I had a nagging feeling that he still might show up in person. His secretary, Rose Mary Woods, and others in his office kept calling during the planning, asking how it was going, how many people were coming, and what all was on the schedule.

My suspicions were confirmed around 8 p.m. when the president's Secret Service contingent showed up. Then, a few minutes later, the band struck up "Hail to the Chief."

President Nixon, wearing a tuxedo, walked right up to our table. He bypassed me and Sallie and went right to my grandmother. She popped up out of her chair, planted a kiss on his cheek, and gave him one of her legendary hugs.

The ballroom went up for grabs. Nixon, the supposedly cold

and remote man, beamed with a warm smile and hugged my Mama as if she were his own. The president then stepped to the podium and apologized for his unannounced appearance, saying that he had another engagement, but had decided to drop in and pay his respects.

He credited me for being "tenacious" in fighting for equality of opportunities for minorities, and said other kind things, but for me the best was the look on my grandmother's face when he said, "I was delighted to meet his grandmother tonight. She really looks like his mother . . . or his sister, for that matter."

It was a corny line, I know, but my grandmother reveled in all the attention she received that night, and rightly so. This event never would have occurred if Miss Nellie Brown hadn't taken me in all those years ago, and filled me with her love and wisdom. She was a humble woman from humble origins, but she multiplied her gifts and passed them on to me, while making sure I made the most of them.

This wasn't my night. It was Mama's. At one point, Nelson Rockefeller came up and gave her a hug and welcomed her. She turned to me and said, "Lord have mercy, Bobby, God is good! You know He guided us from where we came, to where we are on this night! Man had nothing to do with this. God ordained this!"

She got no argument from me. I simply did what she'd taught me. I put my hand in God's hand and He showed me the way.

Chapter 14

FRIENDS ON THE ENEMIES LIST

I F THE PRESIDENT OF THE UNITED STATES IS YOUR BOSS, and he's running for reelection, you are expected to work on his campaign in one way or another. In the spring of 1971, I got a call telling me I'd been put in charge of all efforts to raise funds and bring in black votes for Nixon's 1972 presidential campaign.

The president's top strategists didn't believe Nixon could win more than 10 percent of the black vote. I told them we could get double that if we hit the streets and talked about all that we'd done for them in the last two years.

My team was a division of the Committee to Reelect the President, which had the unfortunate acronym CREEP. We preferred not to be known as the "Black CREEPs" so we came up with another name. We called ourselves the "Black Blitz Team," or the BBT.

One of the Black Blitz Team's goals was to counter the bad press and outrage among civil rights leaders who attacked Nixon's so-called Southern strategy. This program has been portrayed by many critics as an effort to win white Southerners over to the Republican Party by appealing to racists and segregationists. That was not the case.

We wanted to win over all Southerners, white and black, to Nixon's campaign. Nixon's political advisors formed the strategy to appeal to Southern whites *and* Southern blacks who felt they'd been cut out of government programs. There was no intention to prey upon white Southern racial prejudice, though many political analysts decided this was one of the goals of the Southern strategy.

Nixon's foes said he always took a tough law-and-order stance in order to snuggle up to pro-segregation Southern Democrats and Northern blue-collar whites worried about crime, race riots, and declining property values. My mission was to counteract that narrative as much as possible, and to show proof that Nixon's administration had done more for black folks than any previous administration.

We countered the bad press with our own press. We put together a special four-page newspaper section called "Partners in Progress." On the front of it was a photograph of President Nixon surrounded by photos of a few of his black appointees, including me. On the inside pages were 240 photographs of blacks serving in every government position imaginable, from generals and admirals to U.S. ambassadors and department directors.

The Democrats raised hell immediately, which I knew they would do, saying that some of the people were holdovers from previous Democratic administrations. My response was that we could have fired them, which was commonly done in presidential transitions, but we didn't, and now they worked for us. They were obviously competent people, or we would not have retained them.

Inside the special section, we created an illustrated diagram listing many of the programs and initiatives that benefited blacks and their communities. We printed more than a million copies of the Partners in Progress newsletter and then trucked them to black neighborhoods throughout the country during the 1972 election campaign. There were fears that Nixon might get as little as 4 or 5 percent of the black vote in 1972, after getting just 12 percent in 1968. But as it turned out, we brought in nearly 20 percent.

I had every right to be proud of my work for Nixon's reelection campaign, but in truth it was the beginning of the end of my association with him. And, as history has recorded, my White House tenure became a detriment to my business rather than a blessing, at least for several years after a historic scandal broke.

WHILE MANY OF US were working hard on the high road of the campaign trail, it turned out that others were playing dirty on the low road. They created a scandal that would tarnish the Nixon presidency and the reputations of everyone associated with it, including me.

It has been well documented that during the 1972 presidential campaign there were illegal activities conducted by some of Nixon's campaign staffers. Not *all* of his team, mind you. Many of us were kept in the dark about the worst activities. Still, there were things I witnessed during the campaign that turned my stomach. I always grew uneasy when the discussion during campaign meetings changed from "Let's help our friends" to "Let's screw our enemies."

I hadn't come to the White House to take revenge on anyone. I was there to try to do some good. So were most of the other people I knew, though some very good folks got sucked into the mess that became known as Watergate.

When I first learned about the "Responsiveness Program" within CREEP, I was repelled. Later the media would call this part of the campaign the "enemies list." That was a fair description. It was a loosely kept, ever-changing list of people who had openly opposed Nixon, his candidacy, and his presidency.

Everyone on the campaign leadership team was asked to submit names. The idea was then to see if anyone on the list was getting any sort of federal grants or loans that could be cut off. There was also talk of having the IRS and other enforcement groups check into the tax records and activities of the "enemies."

I wasn't naive. I'm sure that every political officeholder, from mayors to public works directors, have some sort of policy, informal or formal, that says, "We help those who have helped us, and we don't do any favors for those who have tried to cut our throats." Still, I tried to excuse myself as quickly and as diplomatically as possible whenever the subject came up.

I had no interest in playing that game, but there were those who tried to recruit me. At one point during the 1972 campaign, George Bell, who worked down the hall as staff assistant for Nixon's special counsel Charles Colson, presented me with a list.

"Take a look at these. This is your part of the enemies list. People have recommended these names. See what you think," he said.

I put the list in my briefcase without looking. Later, with the door closed in my office, I read through the names. Many of them were friends of mine, black and white—good people whose only sin was that they'd dared to criticize the Nixon administration. I was disgusted and embarrassed to have it in my hands.

I had worked with some of those people in my civil rights years. Others were people I respected, even if we had our political differences. George wanted me to go through the list and see if there were any names I wanted to add or take off. The thought of putting them up for scrutiny and maybe even harassment or financial harm made my stomach turn.

I don't recall all of the names on my version of the infamous enemies list. Since then I've seen reports that the list included all twelve of the blacks then serving in Congress, plus Ralph Abernathy, Bayard Rustin, Huey Newton, Marquis Childs, Carl Rowan, and Dick Gregory.

I scanned the names briefly and then locked the list in my office safe. In the days that followed, George and other people in CREEP asked me about the list repeatedly. George called me on the interoffice line once. "Bob, what are you doing with the names I gave you?"

I told him I was planning to get to it. I couldn't believe Nixon really wanted us spending time on such foolishness. The president said a lot of things in anger that I didn't take seriously. Most of those close to him knew to disregard what he said in his darkest moods. I think he trusted that they would ignore him, but there were men around him who thrived on this sort of thing. They played to Nixon's darker side and used his powers to further their own agendas. Some argued that this sort of thing was done in all administrations. "You've got to know who is against us and who is with us," the argument went. "You don't hand out contracts and grants and subsidies to people who are stabbing you in the back."

I didn't buy any of those arguments. I had seen the desire for revenge destroy far too many people. No good could come of it. I'd spent my life channeling my anger into a positive force, and I wasn't about to abandon my principles.

A few weeks after I'd been handed the black enemies list, I walked into the bathroom down the hall from my office and found George Bell there. He was using the urinal. I took the one next to him.

"Bob, you haven't gotten back to me on that list. Did you check it out?" he asked.

"I haven't had time to deal with it, George," I said. "I've been on the road working on the campaign. I'll get back to you later."

George was an affable guy. He took the hint that this was not something I was interested in doing. I never heard another word from him about it, which was a good thing.

After our bathroom discussion I went to my office, pulled the list out of my file, and tore it up. Then I washed my hands of it, literally and figuratively.

IN THE WEEK OF June 19, 1972, I was scheduled to have lunch with Jeb Magruder, the deputy director of CREEP. We'd planned to talk about campaign matters, but Jeb called on the morning of our appointment to say he didn't have time for lunch with me.

"I'm coming to the White House, though, so can we chat a few minutes outside the West Wing? I'm leaving my office now."

He walked over from CREEP headquarters across Pennsylvania Avenue, and I met him on the White House driveway. We talked while leaning against the wall of the West Wing.

Jeb was despondent.

"I'm going through a terrible time right now," he said glumly.

I'd read about and heard the reports of a burglary at Democratic headquarters in the Watergate complex over the weekend. I asked Jeb if his problems were related to that. He said they were.

"It's a tough situation; I don't know what is going to happen," he said.

I commented that the press reports so far didn't make much of it. "Do you think there's more to it?" I asked.

"You don't want to know," Jeb said. "Don't even ask me about it, Bob, because you really, really don't want to know."

I didn't ask any more questions. In the days that followed, it seemed like Jeb had overreacted. The story did not get big play in the press. Reporters seemed more interested in the prospect of added price controls on food items, and the Supreme Court rulings on desegregation and capital punishment. Because some of the burglars caught at Watergate were Cubans, there was speculation in the newspapers that they were looking for information on the Democrats' plans for relations with Cuba.

There was, however, one very strange story related to the break-in. It was a wire service report about Martha Mitchell, whose husband, John, was head of Nixon's reelection campaign. Wire service reporter Helen Thomas wrote that she'd received a bizarre telephone call from Martha, who'd claimed that John was holding her prisoner in a cottage somewhere.

Sallie and I had always enjoyed Martha at social events. She was a live wire, without any pretense at all. She often sought Sallie out at Washington social functions, and they'd spend hours talking. Martha was known for her zany charm and her tendency to drink too much.

She'd apparently had a few drinks and then told the veteran reporter that her husband had become upset about the arrests of the burglars at the Democrats' headquarters. Thomas reported also that Martha might leave her husband unless he got out of politics, because it was "a dirty business."

When the reporter asked John Mitchell about his wife's phone call, he told her that Martha was just a little upset with him because of the demands of his job, but that he loved her.

That story seemed to stir things up more, but the Watergate break-in still felt like small potatoes in light of the other big events of the day. In the polls, Nixon was well ahead of the Democratic Party's leading candidate, George McGovern. The Democrats appeared to be fragmenting badly after a chaotic national convention. Our old civil rights nemesis, Governor George Wallace, was talking about forming a third party, and Secretary of the Treasury John Connally, a Democratic stalwart who'd been shot while riding in JFK's ill-fated Dallas motorcade, came out for Nixon.

All of that seemed to put the Watergate burglary stories on the back burner. Two young *Washington Post* reporters, Carl Bernstein and Bob Woodward, were among the few still writing about it. They managed to dig up a few stories concerning dirty tricks and secret campaign funds, but Nixon's efforts to end the war in Vietnam dominated the news up to the November 7 election.

Apparently, those of us who worked on his campaign did our jobs well despite all of the distractions. Nixon won by the greatest margin in history, with 60.7 percent of the vote. More significantly for my part of the campaign, he blew out his opponents in the South and carried nearly 20 percent of the black vote. It had been seen as an impossible task.

SHORTLY AFTER the election, Nixon asked everyone on his staff to submit a resignation so that he could reorganize for his next term. It was standard practice and most people felt they'd be asked to stay with his administration, though maybe in different positions.

I was more than ready to bow out and get back to my own business. I had struggled financially through most of my White House tenure. My salary was never more than $40,000, a hefty cut from the $100,000 a year or more I'd earned with my public relations firm.

I was supporting my grandparents and my mother, who'd moved back in with them in High Point after being diagnosed with breast cancer. Because of taxes and other expenses on properties I owned, I'd gone through most of my savings. I'd had to take out loans to get by.

Many family members, friends, and acquaintances assumed I was knee-deep in money since I worked at the White House. Some asked for loans, or handouts. I had too much of my grandmother in me to turn anyone away.

A few days after Nixon was reelected, I turned in my resignation. On November 29, President Nixon had Bob Haldeman call me to join him at Camp David. I flew out in a White House helicopter.

We convened around an enormous fireplace in Nixon's cabin and talked like old friends. This time, he knew I was serious about quitting. He complimented me for helping him on many fronts. Late in our conversation, the president said he wanted to reward me for my work and loyalty.

"What do you want to do, Bob? Do you want to be an ambassador? How about a top job on the domestic side?" Nixon asked.

I told him that I wasn't looking for another government job. He then asked me to send him some recommendations for ambassador positions, to reward campaign supporters. Nixon said I should come up with a list of countries I'd like to visit, and then he'd make my friends the ambassadors of those countries so I'd have a connection to each of them. After all these years, I'm still not certain whether he was kidding about that or not.

Next, Nixon asked who I thought should replace me as a presidential assistant. I told him that I'd get back to him with that. Later I recommended my close friend from Atlanta, Stanley Scott, who had introduced me to Wyatt Walker and Dr. King. I'd brought Stan to the White House earlier as an assistant director in the White House Office of Communications, since he'd been a newspaper and television reporter.

The only thing I asked for myself in that final meeting as Nixon's assistant was continued access to him, so that if I had clients who wanted to get messages to him I could provide that service. He said there would be no problem with that. The president also told me to hang on to my special White House pass.

"All you have to do is get in touch with one of the guys here and tell them you are going to come and see me," Nixon said. "Of course, I'll want to be able to call you if I need something too."

I told President Nixon that there would be no problem with that either. Later, we rode back to the White House together in his helicopter. A few weeks after I'd cleared out my office and returned to private life, I received a kind note from him thanking me for my four years as his special assistant. It read, in part: "You played a key role in helping us propose, develop and implement programs for the minorities of our country, and you did so with the greatest sensitivity and distinction."

I appreciated his words, but I was eager to move on with my life. My exit strategy called for opening a Washington, DC, office to make use of the many contacts I'd made in government and business. I had some catching up to do financially, but the future seemed promising, thanks to all the high-level connections I had made in government and the business world.

I'd always told President Nixon that I was willing to do anything he asked me to do, as long as it did not violate my own principles, personal beliefs, or the law. Nixon agreed to my terms and kept his promise to me throughout my time with his administration. I left before the storm broke, but I did not escape its wrath.

Chapter 15

LIFE IS NOT A SMOOTH RIDE

SHORTLY AFTER NIXON WON HIS SECOND TERM, DICK GREG-ory, the comedian turned activist, showed up unannounced at our Washington, DC, apartment. This was before I'd left the White House. It was late Saturday morning, and Sallie and I were enjoying a rare day of relaxation.

"I need to talk with you," he said.

He sounded upset, but you never knew with Dick. He was a brilliant guy in many ways, but also highly eccentric. I'd known him as a fan since the early 1960s when Sallie and I lived in New York City; we'd caught his comedy act at the Village Vanguard and other nightclubs.

He was starting out as a raucous comedian then, but he quickly became one of the top satirists of his era. Dick was the only man who could make racism humorous in those tumultuous times. He used the word "nigger" back when using that term was like light-ing a fuse, but he turned racial prejudice into such an outrageous concept that he'd have black and white people rolling in the aisles together.

Dick became a more serious social commentator during the civil rights era, often walking side by side with Dr. King during demonstrations. He was arrested many times and once severely beaten in a Birmingham jail. He appeared at fund-raisers for the SCLC and the Student Nonviolent Coordinating Committee, and also contributed heavily to the movement, sometimes chartering planes and flying in food for poor blacks in the Deep South.

In 1968, Dick ran against Nixon as the Freedom and Peace Party's candidate, picking up 47,000 votes. He was a man of extremes. He'd gone from being seriously overweight to a rail-thin health food advocate. He staged long fasts to bring attention to human rights issues, but he also embraced conspiracy theories of all kinds.

Some people thought Dick was off the wall, but I'd found him to be a thoughtful, interesting guy—and always worth listening to. Dick had a wise, almost mystical quality, and even his wildest theories had elements of truth to them. Unlike so many others, he refused to condemn me for taking the White House job. He understood that I was working with Nixon to move the civil rights agenda forward.

"Keep doing what you are doing," he'd say on the occasions when I saw him. "I know you are catching hell, but keep it moving, man. We love you, brother."

On that day in 1972, Dick blew through the front door and into our living room like a missile firing multiple warheads of commentary on the wars in Vietnam and Cambodia, conspiracies, and political intrigue.

Sallie retreated to the bedroom. I couldn't keep up with the monologue, but the focus seemed to be that he had an overpowering sense that the Nixon administration was doomed.

"You've got to get away from them or you'll go down too," he warned me.

I'd been surprised before when Dick's seemingly outrageous predictions proved true, so I didn't laugh him off. I listened carefully.

"You may not believe me about this. I know you all just came off the greatest election victory of any president, but Nixon is not going to serve out this second term," he said.

In truth, the same thoughts had been festering in my mind, and in the minds of many who feared that the persistent rumors of political dirty tricks and black bag operations—not to mention Martha Mitchell's phone calls to the media—were building toward serious scandal.

"I'm telling you, Nixon is going down. He'll either be impeached or forced to resign. Or both," Dick said.

I was shaken by what he boldly put out there. The huge election victory had eased my mind a little over the rumblings about the Watergate burglary, but now Dick had come into my house on a Saturday morning to play the role of black oracle.

Dick was no fan of Nixon's, so maybe this was wishful thinking on his part, I thought.

"What else do you see in your crystal ball?" I teased.

"This is just how my mind works. Things come to me and I can't control the thoughts," he said. "Sometimes things come to me. I can sense a scandal, a big scandal," he said. "You are a good brother and you've done a whole lot of stuff for black people. I don't want to see you go down with this thing."

He went on and on. I told him that I'd be all right. At that point, I'd left Nixon's staff already and returned to my business. But I didn't believe that Nixon would be forced from office, or that he would willingly resign.

I was wrong. Dick Gregory had nailed it, and even though I'd been warned, I was still shocked and hurt.

I'D LEFT BEFORE the Watergate scandal unfolded, but I still was dragged into the investigation. In the summer of 1973, two investigators from the office of Senator Sam Ervin, a North Carolina Democrat, came unannounced to see me in the DC office I'd just opened.

They were two younger guys and they each carried very big briefcases, the kind with belts wrapped around them. They were assigned to the Senate Select Committee on Presidential Campaign Activities, which Senator Ervin chaired. They wanted to know about my role and activities in CREEP, President Nixon's reelection committee.

They were especially interested in the enemies list. They said it had been alleged that I was one of the "key figures" in the program to identify and target Nixon's political foes. I told this two-man fishing expedition that my campaign job was only to win over minority voters.

The investigators didn't seem convinced. Instead they opened their huge briefcases and dramatically began slapping one memo after another on the table. They were memos written by, and to, me by campaign staff members. Many were about campaign matters.

"We have memos here that say nobody was to get a contract or grant from any agency within the Nixon administration unless you approved it, Mr. Brown. We know that there was a quid pro quo that unless a person supported the White House and the Republican Party, he would not receive a grant or federal aid of any kind."

I'd been trying to keep a level head, but I was beginning to get angry at this innuendo. "If that's what you are here for, I want you to pull all the material out of your briefcases right now and show me one shred of evidence you have—one memorandum with my signature from my office—that contains any reference to illegal or clandestine activities. And I'll tell you what: if you've got one, I'll chew it up and swallow it right here and now!"

One of the investigators tried to bluff me. "We have many memos in which your name is mentioned, implying that people had to go through you to get things done."

"That may be true," I countered, "but people can write anything they want. Unless you have proof that I was involved in anything illegal, I suggest you pack up your briefcases and get the hell out of my office now."

The two men looked like contrite schoolboys.

"We didn't mean any harm," one of them said on his way out the door.

I NEVER HEARD from the Ervin committee again, but the Watergate scandal dogged me for many years after. There was testimony during the Watergate hearings that I was one of the key staffers who decided where federal assistance went, and that I had a voice in who was hired for government jobs.

The investigators insinuated that my hiring and funding decisions were made based on politics, which of course was partly true. Politics was a consideration in every decision made in the White House if you valued your job. It wasn't always the primary consideration, though, and I often said to hell with politics and did what I thought had to be done.

My grandmother called my office in a fret during the Watergate hearings. She said people told her my name had been mentioned. She asked if I could possibly go to jail. I told her not to worry about it.

"All I did was help people as much as I could. I have no regrets. And I did nothing wrong."

The same innuendo led to my being subpoenaed later in 1973 to appear for questioning in the office of Senator Lowell Weicker Jr. of Connecticut, an independent-minded Republican who served on Ervin's investigative committee.

I was nervous only because I'd heard that Senator Weicker was being very aggressive. He was no fan of Nixon, but he asked me only two questions, both pertaining to my role in CREEP and whether or not I had any knowledge of actions taken against those on the enemies list.

I wasn't there for more than five minutes. I told him that I'd stayed as far away from the enemies list as possible. That marked the end of my involvement in the investigation, but not in the consequences.

As the investigation gained steam, my office telephone stopped ringing with calls from clients. By the end of 1974 and in early 1975, I was forty years old and struggling to pay the rent. On top of the scandal, a recession had all but shut down business across the country, and public relations contracts are often among the first things cut when corporations fall on hard times.

Feeling pinched, I went to one of the biggest banks in the country for a loan. I called upon an executive. I'd done him a few favors while I was in the White House. I thought it was fair to ask him for help in return.

When I told him the problems I was facing, he curtly said: "I'll see what I can do."

I didn't hear from him for a few weeks, so I called again. His secretary said the bank was sending a representative to speak with me. It was a black fellow, which gave me hope, though he was all business.

"Look, Mr. Brown. I've been looking over your records and your financial affairs and I've done everything I can do. Your situation is so bad I don't see how we can get approval for a loan to you. In my opinion, you should file for bankruptcy."

I told him that if that was his recommendation, then we had no more to talk about. He left and I went back into my office, closed the door, and got down on my knees to pray.

Lord, I am down, down, down. I am willing to go whichever way You want me to go. If You have something You want me to do, I am willing to do it. I don't know which way to turn. I need some guidance, and I need for something positive to happen to give me some light. I've tried everything that I know. I'm lost as to what I should do next.

Hundred-dollar bills did not come raining down from above. The phone did not immediately ring with client calls. Still, I felt a change come over me almost as soon as I finished my prayer and got back on my feet, a sense that things were about to turn for the good. I believe my grandmother's spirit filled me with faith and gave me the strength to persevere.

I still had a few clients, but no cash flow. I couldn't keep up with expenses at that point. I was about $100,000 in debt before things began to slowly pick up. The economy was starting to come back, and the phone began ringing again. But just when things looked hopeful, I had a couple of stumbles.

I partnered with a client who had a food service business and needed help navigating the federal rules and regulations for minority contracts. We spent several months clearing all the hurdles before landing a very nice contract for $860,000 in late 1973.

It was a legitimate deal and a great thing for both my partner and me. Then the media latched onto it and twisted it into something despicable. Syndicated columnist Jack Anderson, an investigative reporter and crusader, did a story in which he portrayed me as a wealthy former Nixon aide who'd created a federal program for disadvantaged minorities and then joined the private sector to capitalize on that same program.

I'd done nothing illegal, immoral, or shady, and I was not wealthy by any means at that point in my life. Anderson wrote several columns portraying me as a criminal, though he refused my invitation to check the records. His columns were hurtful and I paid a heavy price. Because of all the bad publicity, I left the business after less than a year, selling out to my partner, who stayed with it and did well.

My personal life also plunged into a deep valley of despair in this period. Gracie, my natural mother, died from breast cancer in May of 1975. Then, shortly afterward, my grandmother Nellie was diagnosed with the same disease. She was eighty-four years old. She had noticed the symptoms much earlier, but she refused to go to the doctor because she wanted to be there to care for my mother.

My beloved grandmother and guardian, the woman who'd always been my "Mama," died in June of 1976. She was selfless to the end.

All of my life, she had inspired me with her courage, her faith, and her willingness to help anyone within her reach. Not a day went by that I did not call to mind some encouragement or wisdom she'd imparted to me. That did not change.

Miss Nellie was everything to me. Losing her might have brought me down if she had not done such a grand job of building me up. I stayed on my feet, but barely, during this trying period. The only thing emptier than my aching heart was my drained bank account.

I'd had many glorious moments in my life, so I guess I was due for a downturn. My judgment was thrown off by my decline in fortune, and I took on a Carl Byoir client without giving careful consideration to what I was getting into. This client's company had purchased the Sambo's restaurant chain and was trying to overcome criticism that the brand promoted offensive racial stereotypes. Needless to say, I quickly regretted taking on that challenge.

The client had planned to expand the Sambo's chain into New England and other regions, but they ran into major opposition. They wanted me to assess the situation and recommend ways for them to deal with it while still operating their restaurants. I'd had success turning around such negative situations for clients in the past, but this case threw me into a fire when I was already nursing burns.

Within weeks of opening Sambo's restaurants in the Northeast, the company was blasted for promoting racist stereotypes by the National Urban League and other organizations. I tried to remedy the tense situation by getting the owners to hire blacks for key positions. They put two on their board of directors and more than forty into management training and franchise ownership, but this was a losing cause.

The Massachusetts attorney general filed suit in federal court to force the company to change the name of its restaurants. The governor of Connecticut, Ella Grasso, announced that she would fight expansion of the chain in her state, and towns across New England refused to allow franchises that used the Sambo's name. A reporter for the *Baltimore Afro-American* newspaper interviewed me, and then portrayed me as an Uncle Tom defending a racist company.

You can't expect life to be one smooth ride. The rough times can make you stronger and more thoughtful if you stick to your principles and values. I've learned that you have to be ready for those times, recognize when you've strayed off the path, and self-correct.

I had taken on a bad client in a weak moment. You have to be extremely careful and thoughtful about the business relationships you form. There are times when a client is in such deep trouble that you risk being dragged down with them. If they won't take immediate action to do the right thing—and the smart thing—you have to cut yourself loose and move on. And that is what I did. In fact, I moved on to an entirely different continent.

PART FOUR

Chapter 16

A RIGHTEOUS CAUSE

MANY UNPLEASANT MEMORIES WERE STIRRED ON MY FIRST visit to South Africa, which by that point was being torn apart by racial conflict. Also, there was no little irony in the fact that a black man who'd spent much of his boyhood shining the shoes of mean-ass white guys would first enter the land of apartheid to tour his client's shoe polish factory.

There were so many unsettling aspects of this trip, including the fact that it felt like walking back in time, into the most dangerous corners of the Jim Crow South. In 1985, more than two decades after the passage of the Civil Rights Act of 1964, I entered South Africa with my client, Robert Elberson, chief operating officer of the Sara Lee Corporation, previously known as Consolidated Foods.

In the years since Watergate, my business had picked up thanks to several large clients like Consolidated. Elberson had pushed for his company to purchase the well-known Kiwi shoe polish brand, and he wanted to check out Kiwi's factories in South Africa while also taking the measure of the volatile political situation in the country. He asked me to come along to help him assess whether his company should remain in South Africa or leave because of the turmoil.

Nearly four decades earlier, the Afrikaner National Party, controlled by the country's white minority, had instituted apartheid rule to diminish the black majority's power. They divided black South Africans from whites and from each other, along tribal lines.

The law forbade interracial marriages and sexual relations. It also removed blacks from 80 percent of the nation's land. Millions of black South Africans were forced out of their rural homelands, which were turned over to white owners, and millions more were uprooted and forced to live in shacks in ghetto townships. Apartheid also instituted its own version of Jim Crow, banning blacks from voting, and creating segregated public facilities.

At first, black resistance to these racist government regulations was similar to the civil rights movement in the United States. People waged nonviolent demonstrations, protests, and strikes. But as the white government used increasingly violent measures to control the black majority, the resistance responded with its own violent actions.

In the early 1960s, black leaders, including Nelson Mandela, who founded the military division of the African National Congress, were arrested and imprisoned. Mandela, a lawyer, proved to be a charismatic figure even while in prison.

Owing to pressure from around the world, the country's white president, P. W. Botha, offered to release Mandela and other black nationalist leaders in February of 1985, but only if they renounced violent opposition to apartheid and agreed to obey the country's strict internal security laws.

Mandela declined the offer, saying that he would not "sell the birthright of the people to be free" just to attain his own freedom. The anti-apartheid leader said he would accept freedom only if Botha legalized the African National Congress, released all political prisoners, allowed exiles to return, and committed to ending apartheid. Botha did not accept Mandela's terms. The ANC leader's continued incarceration triggered protests around the world. The white-led government was denounced by the United Nations while embargoes and economic sanctions were leveled against South Africa by the United Kingdom, the United States, and other countries.

Apartheid was much more in-your-face than the Jim Crow racism of my youth, and the violence was much more overt and widespread because the white minority was so afraid of losing its grip on the throats of the black majority. The white government's security forces routinely slaughtered black protestors. They kidnapped, tortured, and killed leaders of the ANC and other black opposition organizations.

The ferocity of South Africa's racism was all the more striking to me because, in the four previous years, I'd spent a great deal of time working and living in Nigeria, a nation then under military rule but also one where blacks ruled themselves. I had first traveled to the country in 1971 on a White House task force sent to investigate the accidental drowning of civil rights leader Whitney Young. While there, I'd made contacts and friends among Nigerians who hoped to one day establish their country's first democratic government.

By the time Nigerians held their first democratic presidential elections in October of 1979, I was back home in High Point. My Nigerian friends contacted me and asked if I would help them set up a democratic system based on the U.S. model.

I spent about four years helping them create their executive and legislative branches. I also helped them write their constitution, and even hired a black North Carolina artist to design their presidential seal.

Sallie had joined me for extended stays in Nigeria. Living there among an almost entirely black population, we both felt as free as we'd ever felt in our lives. We'd spent so much time apart over the previous years; our experiences in Nigeria recharged and deepened our love.

After my experiences with the Watergate scandal, I found healing for my soul and spirit in Nigeria. Sallie and I loved the people there, and we embraced their culture. It felt like home to us. When I learned, many years later, that my ancestral roots traced back to that country, I wasn't surprised at all. No wonder living and working in Africa was such an invigorating and meaningful experience for us.

While living in Nigeria, I had become accustomed to moving unhindered across all levels of society. Shortly after I arrived on my first trip to South Africa in 1985, however, I was reminded that the rules of daily life for blacks there were much different.

I went to check in at the front desk of a hotel in Durban, a major harbor and industrial city on the east coast, with Sara Lee's Bob Elberson. It had been many years since I felt the full force of racism, but my radar was still functioning. The hotel clerk, who was of Indian descent and even darker-skinned than me, glared as I approached the front desk. His back stiffened and he folded his arms across his chest. The hairs on the back of my neck rose. My racist-detector was still finely tuned after so many years of traveling in the Southern United States during the civil rights era.

I felt the hotel reception area shrink around me like plastic wrap.

Bob Elberson, who was white, must have been prepped to handle this situation. He stepped up and began speaking to the surly clerk.

"We've already worked this out. Mr. Brown is an American with our company."

The clerk shuffled through some papers, tightened his lips, and pushed a registration sheet toward me. "Very well, we will allow Mr. Brown to check in."

It was the first of many signs that South Africa in 1985 was worse than Birmingham in 1962. The old rage welled up in me again, but I reminded myself that I was there on business, not as an activist. I calmed myself and went to bed.

After a restless night, I awakened early and decided to walk on the beach across the street from the hotel to settle my nerves. I'd gone only about thirty feet when I was confronted by a large sign that marked the boundary between the BLACKS AND COLOREDS ONLY beach area and the WHITES ONLY area. The familiar sick feeling returned and a question hit me like a shot: *Why am I here?* I thought. *Why am I dealing with this again?*

I'd fought this fight. I wasn't sure I had any interest in revisiting the ugliness I'd experienced in the American South. Later in the day, I toured the Kiwi plant with Bob Elberson and saw apartheid at work on the factory floor. There were a whole lot of white folks working as supervisors and managers, and operating machinery in the skilled, higher-paying positions. I saw some black people too, but they were mostly sweeping the floors and cleaning the restrooms. All of this in a country where the overwhelming majority of the population was black.

I turned to Bob Elberson and said what I would later say to all the top people in his company, and at Kiwi: "This situation is nothing but trouble. We have to change this, because they are the majority here, and they will one day rise up against you unless you let them share in the rewards and the power. We need to make changes fast by hiring and promoting more blacks, and we need to monitor the progress and stay on top of it."

On that first trip, many of the blacks who were working as janitors were reluctant to talk with me. They called me "sir" and averted their eyes, as if not sure what to make of a black man in a business suit and in the company of white executives.

Then I met with several workers who were not afraid to express themselves. Despite the repressive government, they valued their jobs as an opportunity to better their lives. They sensed that change was coming and that apartheid would eventually give way to pressure from around the world. They were worried, however, about losing what they had managed to gain. Talking to them fortified me. The human drive to create a better life, even under the most adverse circumstances, is a powerful force. I vowed to help them in any way I could.

AFTER THE TOUR, we sat in on a presentation to Kiwi's South African board of directors by a young black man representing a pension management firm. I'm not certain why they wanted us to hear the pitch, but I was impressed by this dynamic go-getter, whose name was Max Maisela. He was the only black working for this pension management company in South Africa. He later told me that they'd made him a "consultant" rather than a full-time employee because they were cautious about having a black man on staff.

After he'd made his presentation and left the room, I told Bob Elberson that he should encourage the local company president to do business with Max. I said Max seemed like the sort of person the company should associate with. It would be good for the company's image and lift the spirits of their black workers to establish a relationship with a black man determined to overcome racial barriers.

Bob Elberson said he'd been impressed with Max too. He directed the head of the local company to go ahead and sign an agreement with Max. At the end of the meeting, I pulled the young man aside and asked him about his background.

"I live in Soweto," he said. "My company flew me in to meet with you. I think they wanted you to see that they have hired a black man. I've only worked with them a short time, but I've had to struggle to get a job that was not in the mines. So I am very happy to have a deal with you, because I don't think they were expecting me to succeed."

I saw a lot of my younger self in Max. I'd had that same hunger and drive at his age.

"We are here to assess the political situation in South Africa," I said. "I will be journeying to Soweto and Johannesburg in the next few days. Would you serve as my guide, so I can see the true situation for blacks here? I want to see what your lives are like, and I don't think the white bosses will give me a true picture."

Max took me into a world that was impoverished beyond anything I could have imagined. On my first visits to Soweto and other black townships of South Africa, I broke down and cried. People were forced to live in the worst kind of conditions you could imagine. There were more than 700,000 impoverished blacks packed together in Soweto, where the air was thick with black smoke from coal and wood stoves.

Most of the residents had been uprooted from cities and suburbs and forced to move into this squalid suburb of Johannesburg. They lived in government-built bungalows, shacks, and huts that were little more than tin or plywood sheets lashed together. Only a small percentage had electricity, about half had cold water, but few had inside bathrooms. In many areas, human waste flowed through open sewers in the streets.

Even in this impoverished community, though, there was a thriving section of busy shops offering canned goods, fruits and vegetables, used furnishings, and other supplies. A few of the shopkeepers were white, but most were black. Despite segregation and the racist government, the entrepreneurial spirit of these oppressed South Africans had stayed strong.

No wonder Soweto had become the center of the anti-apartheid movement. Nelson Mandela, the movement's most prominent leader, had lived in Soweto before being imprisoned in 1962 for treason. His wife Winnie, daughters Zindzi and Zenani, along with other family members, were still living there in a small house.

In June of 1976, South African police began shooting at a group of Soweto's black students who were protesting laws requiring them to learn and use the white Afrikaner language. More than 170 were killed in the weeks and months of rioting that followed. This became known as the "Soweto uprising," and triggered worldwide condemnation of apartheid.

When I visited Soweto, nine years after the uprising, it remained a volatile and tense place. Huge armored Casspir military vehicles and tanks with armed soldiers patrolled the streets. The black residents were under constant scrutiny, and their movements in and out of the township were restricted. I don't know how they carried on their daily lives under such repressive conditions.

Patience Maisela, my friend Max's wife, ran a small, city-owned library. She and Max became my guides to the country, its people, and its problems. My friendships with the Mandelas, Maiselas, and other black South Africans, and my work on behalf of American business clients there, gave me a unique perspective into the impact of apartheid on the lives of the oppressed. I wanted to help the blacks of South Africa break free of the oppressive and racist white government. I came to believe that the only way to spare South Africans from an otherwise unavoidable civil war was to free Mandela, change the authoritarian white-majority government, and hold free, democratic elections.

While many around the world wanted to punish South Africa's government by bringing tough sanctions and shutting down U.S.-owned factories there, I thought that would only hurt the millions of poor black workers we were trying to help. After all, these factory jobs were much better than most available to blacks in the country. I thought foreign governments should find other ways to apply pressure to end apartheid.

My opinions didn't hold much sway. By the summer of 1986, the U.S. House of Representatives had voted for "shock treatment" sanctions, including a trade embargo. All public and private U.S. investments in South Africa were to be terminated.

It was during that same summer, however, that I received a totally unexpected call from an assistant to President Reagan—a call to return to government service in the very country I'd come to care for so much.

"Mr. Brown, I've been asked to inform you that President Ronald Reagan intends to nominate you to serve as U.S. ambassador to South Africa."

My initial reaction to this news was wariness. Although members of Congress had been pressuring him, President Reagan hadn't been a strong opponent of apartheid or the white-controlled government in South Africa. His White House chief of staff, Donald Regan, set off my alarms when he contended that women in America would be upset if they couldn't get diamonds from South Africa.

I felt torn about the nomination, but I was told that this was a call to duty, not a request. I agreed to be interviewed and briefed for the job, but I made it clear I would not enforce policies I did not believe in. I wasn't very diplomatic, which posed problems for my nomination to be an ambassador.

Sallie had her own thoughts on the potential job offer.

"Robert, I have no interest in moving to a country run by racists where white people can tell me where I can and cannot go, and what I can and cannot do." Her assessment sure didn't improve when television, radio, and newspaper reporters began showing up at our doorstep to interview me.

"I can't go out to get the mail without tripping over a newsman," she complained.

As it turned out, my nomination was becoming a major point of controversy beyond our family. Many black Democrats and civil rights leaders opposed my nomination because they didn't like Reagan's policies. Other critics came out of the woodwork, saying I was too pro-business and anti-union, and all sorts of other nonsense. I should have expected it. When you spend most of your life trying to bring warring groups together for the greater good, you tend to draw a lot of fire from people who have something to lose if a resolution is reached.

After several days of briefings and meetings with State Department and White House officials, it became clear that the administration expected me to toe the line and follow orders from Washington, rather than create policies and enact strategies to bring an end to apartheid.

This wasn't what I wanted. I preferred to work quietly and out of the line of fire. I hadn't sought out the ambassador position, and I didn't have the time or the patience to put up with baseless allegations and petty slander.

Three days into the madness, I drafted a letter to President Reagan withdrawing my name from nomination. This pleased Sallie beyond measure, because it meant the small army of reporters camped out in our front yard would disperse.

In a farewell interview, one of them asked me whether I would continue to be involved in South African affairs. "Oh yes, I'll be going back, I'm sure," I said.

With a vengeance, as it turned out.

I HAD DECLINED the ambassador post, but within a short time I was drawn even more deeply into South Africa's affairs. This next major moment in my life began with another phone call—this one from an old friend from the civil rights era.

I was back in High Point in 1986, still working to rebuild my public relations business, when my friend Coretta Scott King, widow of the Reverend Martin Luther King Jr., called with a request.

"Bob, I've been invited to go to South Africa," she said. "I've never been there. Will you go with me?"

Coretta had been invited to speak at a summit meeting of the

Commonwealth of Nations in Harare, Zimbabwe. She also wanted to attend a ceremony inducting the 1984 Nobel Peace Prize recipient, Bishop Desmond Tutu, as the first black archbishop of the Anglican Church.

Coretta was active in the anti-apartheid movement in the United States, having been arrested during a demonstration in Washington, DC. She was eager to see South Africa for herself. The country was on the verge of civil war. Protests and violence had escalated.

She was hoping to use her trip to South Africa to arrange a meeting with President Botha to lobby for Mandela's release. She also planned to request a meeting with Mandela himself. She saw Mandela as South Africa's counterpart to her late husband. Both advocated nonviolent resistance to racial discrimination and injustice.

The only problem was that the South African government required approved visas for everyone visiting the country. Those were tightly controlled. Very few outsiders were granted them. Fortunately, I had met the South African ambassador to the United States at a prayer breakfast in Washington. I called him and asked him to grant the visas to Mrs. King, her small delegation, and me. A few days later, the ambassador called and told me we'd all been approved for the visas.

Later, we learned there were warring factions even within the South African anti-apartheid movement—and one of the few things all of them agreed on was that they didn't want outsiders from the United States interfering with their fight.

Our first stop in South Africa was Cape Town, for the festivities surrounding Bishop Tutu's investiture as archbishop. Before the service, Coretta met with a group of South African anti-apartheid leaders who were troubled when they learned that she planned to meet with President Botha. They advised us that neither Bishop Tutu nor Winnie Mandela felt it was a good idea. Later we met with Tutu and he expressed his feelings in person.

"Apartheid is evil and insidious," he said. "It has damaged our country terribly. We need your support. Meeting with Botha would send the wrong message."

Because of their objections, we backed off. Instead, Coretta wrote a letter urging Botha to release Mandela and end apartheid. I delivered the letter to Botha's aides privately at their Cape Town office. It was a tense situation. Their offices were guarded by armed military police. I had called to arrange the meeting, so an aide met me at the main entrance. When I arrived, he delivered an unexpectedly warm message from President Botha: "The president sends his regrets to Mrs. King and hopes they will have a chance to meet sometime in the future," he told me.

Within a few hours of announcing our decision to cancel the meeting with President Botha, there came an invitation to Mrs. King from Winnie Mandela. She asked Coretta to come meet with her at her home in Soweto.

At that point, neither Coretta nor I had met Mrs. Mandela, so we gladly accepted the invitation. Winnie Mandela had a dramatic presence in those days: striking, proud, and intelligent, the sort of revolutionary figure who inspires novels. She often wore flamboyant styles ranging from headbands, turbans, and berets to Zulu tribal wear, colorful dresses with pan-African prints and wild animal prints.

She was also extremely controversial, even among those in the anti-apartheid movement. There were widespread reports that Mrs. Mandela was becoming increasingly militant. She'd even taken to wearing the coats and pants of a soldier. Just a few months earlier, she'd made comments that appeared to endorse the use of burning tire "necklaces" against the black opponents of the African National Congress.

She lived humbly back in her Soweto days. When Coretta and I arrived at her one-level redbrick home with a corrugated tin roof, she welcomed us into her living room, which had rugs scattered across the concrete floors. Coretta and Winnie discussed the similarities in the lives of their husbands as freedom fighters in their respective countries. "What is right will prevail because God wills it," Mrs. King told Mrs. Mandela.

Winnie was touched by those words. She told Coretta that Dr. King's victories in the United States had been an inspiration to her husband and to black South Africans.

Mrs. Mandela then shared that she and Nelson had long wanted their elder daughter, Zenani, and her husband to attend college in the United States, but she didn't know how to accomplish that. Other Americans had said they could arrange it, she said, but no one had followed through. Winnie was forbidden by the white government leaders to leave South Africa, even though her children and their children with Swaziland passports could travel wherever they wished.

Winnie said Zenani, then twenty-seven, wanted to study political science; and her husband, Prince Thumbumuzi Dlamini of Swaziland, wished to pursue an American law degree.

I was still processing that information when Coretta said to Mrs. Mandela: "Mr. Brown here has been one of our big supporters over the years, and he has many contacts."

Then Coretta turned to me and said, "Bob, do you think you could help arrange this?"

I said yes without hesitation—and without giving a lot of thought as to what I was getting into. It did occur to me that my High Point friend Ron Carter might be helpful. He worked as dean of students at Boston University, and I knew he admired Nelson Mandela a great deal.

Mrs. Mandela later sent me a letter authorizing me to act as the family's representative in the United States, and with the assistance of Dr. John Silver, president of Boston University, went far beyond the norm to ensure that every required document needed to facilitate the Mandelas' U.S. arrival was secured. Dr. Carter actually traveled to South Africa to prepare the family for the transition to the United States and Boston University. In the seven and a half years that followed, I paid for their back-and-forth travel to the United States and their Boston rental house, and I provided them a vehicle while also covering their monthly expenses.

I was only trying to be helpful, but as a result of my efforts to help Mrs. Mandela and her children, I soon found myself being drawn into the family's inner circle, and into the fight to win Nelson Mandela's freedom.

ABOUT SIX MONTHS after my first visit with Mrs. Mandela, I returned to South Africa on business. While there, I called Winnie to talk about her daughter and son-in-law. She invited me to again visit her in Soweto and I accepted.

I'd hardly walked into the house for that visit when she stunned me with an invitation that I had never expected.

"Nelson wants to meet you," she said. "Can you travel to see him in prison while you are here? He said if you are going to be our daughter's guardian in the United States, he wants to know you better."

As far as I'd heard, only family members and his lawyers had been allowed to visit Nelson Mandela in prison—and even then, only on a very limited basis.

"I'd certainly welcome the opportunity to meet him," I said, "but I can't believe the government would allow it."

Winnie gave me a sly smile. "Oh, I think it can be arranged."

I soon learned that Winnie Mandela was a force to be reckoned with. Several days later, the telephone in my Johannesburg hotel room rang at about 10:30 p.m. The director of South Africa's foreign services, Neil van Heerden, informed me that President Botha had approved my visit to see Nelson Mandela for the next day at Pollsmoor Prison near Cape Town.

My next call was to Winnie Mandela. I told her the news, and she was ecstatic. "I told you! I told you!" she said.

The next morning, May 8, 1987, Winnie had her daughter and son-in-law meet me at the airport in Cape Town. Zenani and her husband, Prince Muzi, then rode with me to Pollsmoor Prison, about forty-five minutes away.

"This is so unusual, for the government to allow you to visit my father," said Zenani.

"We just hope it is not some kind of trap," her husband said. "You never know what they might do."

That is what life was like for the Mandela family. Even in their own country, they never knew whom to trust.

The drive through the area around the prison held some surprises for me. I had expected it to be in a bleak, industrial setting, but instead Pollsmoor was surrounded by lush vineyards, wineries, and lovely (white) neighborhoods, whose homes boasted views of distant mountains. It was more like California wine country than the parts of South Africa I'd seen so far. Clearly this was a land of great disparities.

Our driver was scared to travel in this infamous area, so he let us out near the front gate to Pollsmoor Prison. The guards were cordial, which only made us all the more suspicious. We felt like we were being lured into the enemy camp. Racism has that effect. You come to fear that every extended hand holds a knife. I could hear my grandmother's voice say, "I dare you to trust God."

The guard at the gate directed us to walk about half a block to the main building. Again, it was disorienting to see a prison in such beautiful surroundings, especially since I'd been to Rikers Island, the prison just outside Manhattan near LaGuardia Airport—a much more forbidding place.

Another wave of suspicion struck me. What if we really were

being lulled into a vulnerable state? Was this just a plot to kill Nelson's children and me, or maybe the man himself? We walked in silence toward the building. I was thousands of miles from home and felt fully exposed. Yet I was also beside myself with the anticipation of meeting one of the world's great champions of freedom. It didn't seem real.

Nelson Mandela had been imprisoned for twenty-four years at that point. Up to this time, as far as I knew, very few people outside of government officials, Mandela's immediate family, and his lawyers had been permitted to visit him at Pollsmoor. Even then, most were restricted to fifteen-minute visits.

At the main door, a man in an officer's uniform extended his hand and introduced himself as the "chief warden." His welcome and the words that followed made my head spin.

"Mr. Brown, all of us here are very pleased and grateful for what you are doing for the Mandela family. I want you to know that. There's a room on the right-hand side on the corner. You can go in, and Nelson will be brought down shortly. There is plenty of room in there, and I want you to know that you can take as much time as you like."

Prince Muzi and Zenani were flabbergasted. They'd been coming to visit her father for years, and they'd been allowed only fifteen or twenty minutes each time. Nobody had met with him longer than that, they assured me. Nor had they ever been greeted so kindly by the guards and warden.

Honestly, we didn't know whether to make a run for it or weep with excitement. Our confusion ended, however, when a tall and trim figure appeared in the doorway. I had to blink a couple of times to assure myself this was really Nelson Mandela casually walking into the visitors' room.

He stretched out his long, thin arms and wrapped them around his daughter and son-in-law as they rushed to hug him, clinging to him with their eyes closed, smiling even as tears streamed down their faces.

Then, with his arms still around them, Nelson Mandela shifted his gaze to me and said, "Bob?"

"Yes sir, Mr. Mandela," I replied, nearly choking up at the sound of my name.

Nelson Mandela then threw his arms around me and said, "I appreciate what you have done for my children. I'm grateful and I am glad you are here."

Before the visit, some people had told me that this once vital man might be weakened by the cruelty and injustice of his long imprisonment. Mandela was just the opposite. He was thin, yes, but remarkably fit-looking. His kind facial features and humble demeanor gave him a spiritual aura that drew me to him. He carried himself with a regal bearing and the confidence of a natural leader.

We sat together at a small table.

"I am overjoyed that they allowed you to meet with me here," Mandela said. "They've not allowed such a thing before. This is a happy time for me, since Winnie and I have been trying to arrange further education for our children for a long time."

He told Zenani that Sallie and I would be her "parents" in the United States, and that she should always be careful to protect and honor the Mandela family name while living and traveling abroad. It was heartwarming to see how loving he was to his daughter, though he had missed nearly all of her life while imprisoned.

A guard was posted discreetly in a far corner of the room. Yet, Mandela talked freely with Prince Muzi and Zenani about family matters, and then he peppered me with questions about my civil rights activities with the SCLC, Dr. King, and Mrs. King.

"I have access to a radio and some books and magazines, so I know about Dr. and Mrs. King and I understand you worked closely with them," he said. "I admired Dr. King immensely. He was one of the great men of our time. I am sorry that Mrs. King could not get in to see me. I would love to meet her sometime."

Mandela said he wanted to provide me with historical background of the ANC and how his nation had come to be so divided. He described the numerous petitions the ANC had presented to the South African government over many years, asking the white leaders to meet with them to discuss their concerns. They had approached various emissaries and appealed to other governments to push the same message, but they were always ignored by the white leaders of their country.

We also talked about communism that day, because there had been accusations that black leaders in the ANC were serving as a front for communists in South Africa. He denied those reports. His voice hardened as he noted that the whites persecuting black South Africans had no right to tell them whom they could turn to for support as long as it was "open season" on blacks in his country.

"How can a government that kills and jails innocent people and little children at random . . . how can they rightfully ask me to renounce violence without doing the same thing themselves?" he said.

He declared that it was vital for all nations, including the United States, to keep the pressure on the South African government. Equal rights for blacks must be protected by constitutional guarantees, he said.

"All I want to do—all that every black South African wants—is to take our rightful place as citizens in our own country. We do not want to run any white people out. It is their home, just like South Africa is my home. There is room in the country and in our government for both black and white South Africans. We can run the government together, to live together in peace. My country is one of vast and unlimited potential, which can only be fully realized for future generations by all South Africans working together as full citizens politically, socially, and economically," he said.

I found it striking when he talked about how the good white and black people in South Africa needed to come together to resolve the nation's racial division. The white leaders had imprisoned him for more than two decades. They had killed many of his friends. They had tortured and imprisoned his wife. Yet he refused to judge all whites by the sins of the Afrikaners who had imprisoned him. I came away convinced that Mandela was touched by the hand of God.

As Nelson Mandela explained his philosophy of leadership and briefed me on the fight against apartheid, I took notes like a schoolboy, hardly containing my excitement. *How did I even get here? In a prison run by white racists, sitting with this legendary figure, freely talking like old friends? The Lord certainly has walked me into some remarkable situations.*

"You know, Bob, one of the things that is important for us to understand is that South Africa is a beautiful country," he said. "It is a good country, and the only thing necessary to make it a *great* country is for the good white people and the good black people to get together and make it *their* country."

Mandela became more animated and energized as we spoke.

"I am saddened by all of the violence between races and different people here and around the world," he said. "I pray that a peaceful resolution can be found here, so I can take my message of conciliation and hope to other places around the world. I want to forgive my captors for all they've done and help our country move forward. So much needs to be done."

We talked about our shared faith in God. Mandela said he'd long been an admirer of the Reverend Billy Graham, whom I'd met several times. We talked about asking Graham to preach peace in South Africa. He asked me to convey his regards to Rev. Graham and ask for his prayers.

"I believe the church could be a powerful source of change in my country," he said.

I have always considered myself a Christian, but the power of Mandela's faith and forgiveness was humbling and inspiring. And yet, there was nothing soft or weak about him. He was forceful in his beliefs and adamant about the justness of his cause. Mandela said that both sides had made mistakes, but he blamed the intransigence of the white minority for stirring feelings of violence among even the most peaceful of his people.

It was a memorable meeting. Initially I was nervous, but Mandela's warmth made me comfortable. He was an impressive man in many ways: humble, extremely intelligent, and tough-minded. I felt an aching sadness watching Mandela say goodbye to his daughter and son-in-law that day. The injustice of his situation was overwhelming. I walked away more determined than ever to do what I could to help bring about this great man's release and help his family carry on.

Chapter 17

CONFRONTING THE CROCODILE

AFTER THAT FIRST MEETING WITH NELSON MANDELA, I spoke with my friend Arnold Mentz, who was then the economic minister at the South African embassy in Washington. I'd worked with Arnold on behalf of my clients with operations in his country and we'd become close. I shared with him that Mandela had been quite conciliatory in his comments about the white leaders and the apartheid government.

"He seems to be far more interested in moving the country forward than seeking revenge against his oppressors," I told Arnold. "I've already started writing a detailed memorandum about the meeting and Mr. Mandela's comments. I will send it to you tomorrow."

"I think our leaders would be very interested in his position," he replied.

The next day, I sent him a seven-page memo drafted from my notes on the meeting with Mandela. Arnold Mentz forwarded it to the South African ambassador to the United States. He, in turn, sent it on to members of the South African Cabinet and to President Botha.

I sent the memo also to President Reagan and his secretary of state, George P. Shultz, whom I had known in my own White House years.

Arnold told me a few months later that my memorandum was the topic of great discussion and that President Botha himself had called it "eye-opening."

Years later, after a freed Mandela became president of South Africa, Arnold offered an even more remarkable, and gratifying, appraisal: "Bob, your memorandum was the first step to changing the mind-set of the Cabinet members and other decision-makers in favor of releasing Mr. Mandela."

I can't say for certain if that was true. As we later learned, there had been discussions between Mandela and government officials over the years, but history has noted that in May of 1988—almost exactly one year after I met with Mandela that first time and wrote my report on our discussion—the head of the apartheid government's intelligence agency began an intense round of secret meetings with Nelson Mandela to negotiate his release, under the orders of President Botha.

At the time, of course, I had no idea of all this, though I soon picked up on the fact that the white government's attitude toward Mandela was shifting. About six weeks after that first meeting with Nelson Mandela, Winnie did tell me that "there had been some conversations" between her husband and government officials.

"Hopes are brighter for his release than they have ever been since he's been in prison," she told me privately.

IN JULY OF 1988, Mrs. Mandela contacted me again and asked if I would be willing to have another meeting with her husband at Pollsmoor Prison. She said the family was concerned that outsiders were using the Mandela name for personal profit and without permission. Millions of dollars donated for the fight to free Mandela had been misappropriated.

On this return trip to South Africa, I was accompanied by two young black men who were working for me. One of them was Armstrong Williams, a bright twenty-six-year-old who worked in my Washington, DC, office. The other was my tall and thoughtful vice president for business development, Stedman Graham, then thirty-seven years old.

I'd met him and his girlfriend, Oprah Winfrey, through a mutual friend, the writer and poet Maya Angelou, who lived in Winston-Salem, just twenty miles from High Point. Maya had been a friend to Sallie and me for many years. She was like a sister to both of us. In the mid-1980s, Maya introduced us to Stedman and Oprah. The young television show host had grown up reading Maya's books, and when they met during an interview, they bonded. Sallie and I met Oprah and Stedman about a year before Oprah signed on to do her own syndicated television show. At this time, she was still hosting a local program, *A.M. Chicago*, so she wasn't yet a major celebrity.

In the years that followed, Oprah and Stedman became like a daughter and son to Sallie and me. None of us had any idea that they would become such a famous couple, or that Oprah's wealth and influence would become so vast. As her national television show became more and more successful, she looked to us as friends she could relax with.

Stedman and I first bonded over our shared enthusiasm for golf, and once I got to know him well, I asked him to join my public relations business. Stedman was also interested in learning about the volatile situation in South Africa. This trip would prove to be an immersive experience into that country's increasing turmoil.

Violence between white government forces and blacks raged across South Africa. Deadly gun battles between anti-apartheid forces and police and military units occurred almost daily somewhere in the country, which was also increasingly volatile due to a series of bombings of police stations, soccer stadiums, railroad terminals, restaurants, and private homes. There had also been a significant increase in car bombings and grenade attacks throughout the divided nation.

UPON ARRIVAL FOR my second meeting with Nelson Mandela that July of 1988, his wife invited us to join her at a small rally of about thirty people, followed by a party at the home of a journalist who was a friend of Winnie's. The rally was to support a call for freedom for the ailing and elderly Harry Gwala, an imprisoned anti-apartheid leader who'd been a compatriot of Nelson Mandela.

After the rally, we drove to a rural area outside Johannesburg for the party. On the way, we learned there had been a growing number of threats of violence against Mrs. Mandela and her supporters. She had enemies in the white government, of course, but she'd also made enemies among a certain violent black gang when she decided to use a rival gang as her security force.

That night, the party was interrupted when more than a hundred security police were spotted moving toward our location. There were very realistic fears that they might attack and kill us all, given the volatile environment. A call to the U.S. embassy in Cape Town resulted in the security police backing off.

The next morning, we learned that the country house where we'd been for the party had been destroyed by a firebomb late in the night. We also had threatening calls made to our hotel room. During the night, someone had set off a smoke bomb in our hallway.

Stedman and Armstrong were by my side immediately, so I wasn't scared; but I was having flashbacks to Birmingham in the civil rights era.

"You have to always wonder, which way will they come for us if they decide to kill us?" I said to my young friends. "We have to remain calm but vigilant, and we can't trust anyone but ourselves here."

Sallie and Oprah were following developments in South Africa, and both of them demanded that we return home. Oprah offered to send a plane. Stedman, always the loyal and protective friend, told her he wasn't leaving unless I did.

At least some of the threats, we learned, were the result of the rivalry involving Mrs. Mandela's young security guards.

"Bob, you tend to trust people more than I do," Armstrong said. "I am not so sure Winnie isn't using us as pawns in some game we don't understand. This could get dangerous in a hurry."

I knew Armstrong might have had a point. My inclination was to trust people until they proved themselves untrustworthy. Many times, he'd heard me quote my grandmother's saying "You can find good anywhere, and you can do good everywhere." I looked for good in everyone, but sometimes they weren't as good as I hoped.

Winnie Mandela proved that she was a great and loyal friend to Stedman, Armstrong, and me. She'd not only kept the struggle alive while her husband was in prison, she served as our rock and salvation while we were in South Africa. We'd agreed that she was our hero and that we'd love her forever after that.

On July 22, I went once more to Pollsmoor Prison and met with Nelson for the second time, just four days after his seventieth birthday. Mrs. Mandela and Zindzi joined us. This time, Nelson did not look well. His voice had a raspy sound, and he seemed to have trouble catching his breath. A month later, he would be diagnosed and treated for tuberculosis.

Our discussions on this trip were focused primarily on their concerns about the family name being exploited. Nelson was particularly upset about an HBO movie called *Mandela,* starring Danny Glover and Alfre Woodard. It was an unauthorized portrayal of Nelson and Winnie's courtship and relationship. The family had no input, nor did they receive any compensation. I agreed to serve as their representative in guarding the family name from any possible exploitation.

This certainly was not another role or responsibility I sought, but I believed in Mandela's fight for freedom and I wanted to help the family in any way I could. When we left the prison that day, there were reporters from around the world gathered outside. They wanted to know what we had discussed with Mr. Mandela. I stayed in the background and let Winnie and Zindzi do the talking. They gave brief statements, and it appeared that the reporters were satisfied. But then Zindzi said, "Mr. Brown should tell you about the conversation he had with my father about the use of the Mandela family name."

I was on the spot. When the reporters directed their questions to me, I told them only that Mr. Mandela had agreed to grant me power of attorney to protect the use of the Mandela family name and its interests around the world. I also noted that I had agreed to consult with Oliver Tambo, president of the ANC, on all family-related matters.

That was all I said. But the next day there were headlines around the world saying that I had presented myself as the sole guardian of the Mandela name. Some later news accounts also reported that Nelson Mandela himself had refuted my claims and said that I was not authorized by him to do that.

I was shocked. I had no intention to "sell" the rights to the Mandela family's name or to otherwise trade on it. I was never paid, nor was I reimbursed any money that I spent on behalf of the Mandela family—nor did I ever ask to be. Obviously, some faction of the ANC felt that I was somehow usurping their authority. Several days later, a *New York Times* story quoted an anonymous spokesman for the ANC saying, "Mandela is a public figure. His name does not belong to the family but to the movement."

Back home, Sallie was furious. She demanded that I return immediately. "We've got to cut this off. They are trying to ruin your reputation even as you try to help their cause. We can't do this anymore," she said.

———

AFTER THAT MEETING, Stedman and I stayed in South Africa to work with business clients for a week. We were preparing to return home on July 28, 1988, when a hotel bellhop reported that Mrs. Mandela was eager to talk to us.

"There has been a fire. Her house has burned. There are big problems in Soweto," he said.

I called Winnie. "Bob, we have lost everything," she said. "We don't have a single toothbrush left. You must come and help us."

When we arrived, we found an agitated and angry crowd surrounding the blackened remains of the Mandela home. Winnie was on the verge of a breakdown. She kept talking about the "crazy boys" who had burned down her house. There had been a fight that day between her bodyguards and the rival gang members. Nearly fifty teens had thrown stones at the house before setting it on fire.

The Mandela family had lived in this house for more than forty years. They lost everything, including family documents, a piano, wedding and baby photos, and even the last frozen piece of their wedding cake. All of their furniture and clothing was destroyed.

The family had been offered temporary lodging in the home of a friend. Stedman and I went to a local store and bought clothes for Mrs. Mandela and the grandchildren. I sent another friend to pick up food supplies.

When night fell, we feared the gang warfare would erupt again. Gang members were prowling the streets, threatening each other and residents. Winnie asked me to calm things down. Stedman came with me, which was comforting. The young gang members were more likely to listen to a young six-foot-seven former college basketball player than to an older guy like me.

Stedman took one group aside. I took another. We asked the gang members to focus on fighting apartheid instead of each other.

"When you fight and kill each other, it doesn't help you. It helps the whites who want to control you," I said. "You are doing what they want you to do, and it has resulted in the destruction of Nelson Mandela's family home. You need to stop fighting each other and honor Mr. Mandela by focusing on the fight against apartheid, and the fight for his freedom and your own."

They agreed to keep the peace, and it didn't hurt that Stedman and I went out and bought up every bit of fried chicken in the area and provided them with their first good meal in a long time. After making sure that Winnie and the kids were secure, Stedman and I headed back to the United States, where Oprah and Sallie had been waiting and worrying. Winnie Mandela rode to the airport with us to make sure we got there safely.

FOUR MONTHS LATER, I returned alone to South Africa on business and attended a secret meeting that would give us even more cause for concern.

I'd completed my business in Pretoria, and was preparing to leave the next day, when the knock came on my hotel room door. I did not open it. Too many blacks in South Africa had disappeared after such knocks on the door.

My friends in the anti-apartheid movement often warned me about assassins working for the racist white government. They tracked down black activists, dragged them from their homes, tortured and killed them, and disposed of their bodies. Their families would never hear from them again.

I looked through the peephole in the door, saw the badges of the government security force members, and weighed the risks before letting them in. Then they delivered their shocking invitation, repeating it several times; I must have looked as dumbstruck as I felt.

"President Botha would like to meet with you, Mr. Brown."

I had to step back from them, to let my mind wrap around this striking development. If this had been Birmingham in 1963, it would be like getting invited to the KKK headquarters to meet Bull Connor and his boys face-to-face.

I couldn't imagine why the racist leader of South Africa would want to speak with me, unless it was to have me thrown in jail or banned from his country. Yet his security men hadn't threatened me or dragged me out of the room. They'd invited me to meet in several hours with "The Big Crocodile" himself. They knew I'd tell friends where I'd been invited, so it wasn't likely they planned to harm me.

I agreed to meet Botha, figuring that I'd have some time to weigh my options. They instructed me to go to the foreign minister's office that evening. I'd then be taken to the president's suite.

After they left, my first call was to Winnie Mandela.

"You won't believe what has happened to me," I said. "President Botha has asked me to meet with him."

"What does he want?" she asked.

"I have no idea."

"You must meet with him," she said.

Racial violence was escalating throughout the country. Botha and his allies were under intense global pressure even in their own press to end apartheid before a civil war broke out. We knew that. What I did not know in that moment was that representatives of Botha had been meeting with Nelson Mandela in prison since that May. At Botha's request, a team that included his head of intelligence, Niel Barnard, had been conducting a series of secret discussions with Mandela, at first taking his measure and eventually opening negotiations for the terms that would lead to his release.

They were already planning to end apartheid. Mandela had not mentioned a word of this to me, or to anyone else as far as I knew. He'd actually been pushing to meet with President Botha himself.

Unaware of this monumental shift already under way, I went that evening to the State House, where I was greeted by the foreign service director, Neil van Heerden, whom I'd never met in person. I'd expected that he would prep me for my meeting with Botha, but Van Heerden told me that he was as baffled by the president's invitation as I was.

"We didn't even know you were in town until he told us. I would be grateful if you'd debrief me afterwards," he said.

He then walked me to the office of the foreign affairs minister, Pik Botha. He too was disarmingly direct and candid. As he walked me toward the president's office, he said, "I suppose Neil has told you that we do not know why the president wants to speak to you. I would be grateful if you would come back to my office afterwards so I can be debriefed."

That blew me away. The second-highest man in the government didn't know what was going on. At first I had thought they were trying to kill me—now they were asking for my help.

What have I gotten in the middle of now? I wondered. Once again, I found myself inside the "enemy" camp. And again, I could have turned and walked away at any point. Instead, I prayed that God would watch over me, and that some kind of good would come of this meeting.

I kept praying every step of the way toward the office of the fearsome racist leader, who was responsible for untold suffering and death among blacks in his country.

Yet, once more, my grandmother's voice came to me, reminding me that God works in ways we often cannot understand. If God wanted me to meet with President Botha, maybe something good could come of it. P. W. Botha represented the worst of all the racism I'd experienced in my life—everything I'd learned to oppose—but the opportunity to perhaps influence him, or to at least open a door to greater understanding, kept me going.

The foreign minister walked me into Botha's office, and the president, who stood behind his desk, dismissed him. "I want to meet with just Mr. Brown," he said.

Botha was of average height, with a slight paunch, and balding. He wore large-framed glasses. He seemed to be making an effort to appear cordial, but it did not appear to be a natural attitude for him in the presence of a black man. He had the arrogant air of a dictator.

His nickname is appropriate, I thought. *He seems like a predator to avoid if at all possible.*

We shook hands and sat down side by side, about six feet from each other. There was no small talk.

"Mr. Brown, I'm sure you are wondering why I wanted to see you."

"It had crossed my mind," I said.

He told me he was aware that I'd been a frequent visitor to South Africa over the years, that I'd been a candidate for the U.S. ambassador's post, and that I had many friends among black South Africans. Then he asked a question that came as quite the shocker.

"What are your thoughts and ideas about what our government should be doing to end the conflict?"

This was no time to keep my opinions to myself. If the apartheid leader asked what I thought, I was certainly not about to hold back or soft-pedal my views.

I spoke from the heart, telling him that a civil war was imminent unless Mandela was freed and apartheid ended. I noted that isolating and discriminating against blacks hadn't worked in the United States and it would not work in his country either, especially when blacks comprised the vast majority of the population.

President Botha remained silent, though restless, as I spoke. He shifted in his chair several times, signaling that he was not accustomed to allowing blacks to express themselves in his presence. When I insisted that Mandela and Harry Gwala be freed, he raised up in his seat, shook his finger at me, and went into a sort of barely controlled rage. His face turned so red I thought he might burst an artery.

"Mr. Brown, I tried to give that man his freedom and he would not accept it!" he said.

Botha ranted on about Nelson and his refusal to compromise.

"I offered that man his freedom and he turned it down! He was a terrorist against our government, but I was willing to let him go if he renounced violence, but he refused!"

I silently prayed to keep my composure. Botha had imprisoned and likely ordered the deaths of thousands of black South Africans. On the one hand, I was uncomfortable because this very powerful and ruthless man was growling and spewing venom in my presence. On the other hand, I took satisfaction in the fact that Nelson Mandela had obviously gotten the best of his jailer.

Mandela had refused to accept Botha's earlier offer of freedom because of the president's stipulations. I let Botha rage until he paused to catch his breath.

"Mr. President, the Nelson Mandela I've come to know is a proud South African just like you are a proud South African. He wants to see and do the best for this country just like you want to see and do the best for it. He wants unconditional freedom for himself and for his people."

That seemed to calm Botha, just a bit. Perhaps he saw that arguing with me was futile. I sensed that he'd seen the future. World sentiment was building against him.

Abruptly, he rose and thanked me. We'd been talking for nearly an hour.

"I am grateful to you for your observations of Mr. Mandela and I will take them under consideration," he said.

I took one more shot: "If you allow Mr. Mandela to fade away or to be persecuted in some way, or to be killed—or God forbid that he would die a natural death inside that prison—it will bring havoc on this country."

Botha lost it again. He jabbed his hand and chopped the air repeatedly as he railed on about Mandela and his stubbornness. Again he abruptly calmed himself. For a second, I saw a weariness come over him, and a look of resignation. Then he offered perhaps the most striking comment of all.

"We have had some discussion with Mr. Mandela, and we are searching for ways to do this," he said.

I jumped on that statement.

"Your only way out is to free Mandela and embrace democracy," I said.

I was pushing hard against a proud, strong man whose control was waning. I think his bluster and rage had been an attempt to test my resolve, but I never retreated and I never raised my voice to match his.

I doubt that Botha ever viewed black men and women as fellow human beings, let alone equals. I'm not sure he was capable of that; but he did seem to be recognizing that he was fighting a losing battle.

Feeling bold, I took another parting shot. I suggested that he take one small step to ease the grip of apartheid, by dropping the ban on black shoe-shine stands at the airports and hotels.

There were very few ways for blacks in South Africa to earn an independent income. When they'd been banned from shining shoes in the white districts, they'd lost access to cash and to customers who might pay for other goods and services.

I thought this small measure was one he might accept. My goal was to open up jobs for the neediest black families. I'm sure in Botha's eyes shining shoes was subservient work. Yet I knew from my own boyhood experience that shining shoes could help pay the bills, and that this menial job had turned many poor boys into budding entrepreneurs.

Botha said he would consider it, but I didn't hold out hope.

After returning to my hotel, I called Winnie Mandela and told her what had transpired.

"Perhaps something good will come of what has happened," she said.

I was still in South Africa, working with my corporate client, when Winnie called me a few days later. She said Harry Gwala had been set free.

Several weeks later, black shoe-shine boys were allowed back into the white districts. It was a small victory for me, but a great one for those poor kids and their families.

Eight months later, in August of 1989, President Botha resigned from office and F. W. de Klerk was sworn in as acting president of South Africa. Six months after that, Zenani Mandela called me.

"Papa Brown! My father is to be freed! Finally! He will be released from prison!"

The release date was set for February 11, 1990. Zenani was still in Boston with her husband, so she invited me to fly to South Africa with them so we could welcome Nelson Mandela upon his release after twenty-seven years in prison.

Sadly, I had to decline because Sallie was having health problems. Stedman and Armstrong Williams went in my place, making sure Zenani and her husband arrived safely. I don't think either Stedman or Armstrong will ever get over the experience. Stedman had dinner with the reunited Mandela family on the day of Nelson Mandela's release, and then he and Armstrong were invited to join them for breakfast on the morning of his first full day of freedom.

They called me at home to tell me they were having breakfast with Mr. Mandela, and he wanted to speak with me.

"Bob, my friend, I am sorry you can't be here with us to enjoy my first morning of freedom and some very good breakfast," Mandela said.

"I wish I could be there with you all, but my wife has breast cancer and this is a difficult time for her," I said.

"I can understand," Mandela said. "You are in the right place, with your wife. I just want you to know I appreciate everything you have done for my family and my people. I want you to know that I will never forget it."

Mandela called me again when he and Winnie visited the United States for a twelve-day celebration of his freedom. I told him that I was overwhelmed with joy at all that was happening for him and his people. He replied that things appeared to be moving along well, and he added that he wanted to meet with me while he was in Boston on the next leg of his visit.

I accepted his invitation. I had no idea, of course, that I'd be joined by tens of thousands who gathered to greet Mandela in Boston. We did have our own private talk outside the spotlight. Winnie, Zenani, and Zindzi greeted me in their hotel suite when I arrived. We spoke for several minutes, catching up on each other's lives, and then a young man in a suit came into the room and said, "The old man wants to see you now."

Most of the time, Mandela's intimates referred to him as "Madiba," which is an honorary title from his Xhosa ethnic group, so the term "old man" threw me off just a bit, especially since that was the term many of Nixon's top White House aides had used to refer to him.

I shrugged it off and walked into Mandela's room. He stood and greeted me. We hugged and shook hands and then he motioned for me to sit down. He appeared to be very relaxed and in quite good health. We had a private discussion that was very moving. At the end of it, I told him there was no doubt he would make even greater contributions to the world as a free man.

"Well, I don't know about that, but it does seem that everybody wants to meet with me now," he said with a laugh.

THERE HAVE BEEN many wonderful moments in my life, and certainly among them was the experience of that relaxed and private conversation with Nelson Mandela as a free man. Decades of his life and many of his friends had been taken from him, yet he radiated warmth and wisdom. He was truly one of the most naturally charismatic men I've ever known, one of those leaders who made everyone around him aspire to be a more patient, compassionate, and forgiving human being.

THE OTHER PERSON in my life who had that effect on me, of course, was Sallie. Even as I met with Nelson Mandela, my heart was heavy with the knowledge that her health was waning.

Sallie had been diagnosed with the same cancer that had taken my mother and grandmother. By the time I met with the freed South African leader in Boston, she had been undergoing treatment after treatment. She would fight for her life another fourteen years. The cancer would go into remission for a few months or even a year, and then reappear.

I felt helpless. Over the years, I'd worked miracles for my clients, earning a reputation as a problem solver, yet I was clearly no match for Sallie's challenges. I took her to the best doctors I could find, the best clinics across the country. I prayed on my knees, on airplanes, in hotel rooms, in churches wherever I could find them. I held out hope that God would step in and do some healing. This was beyond my power, but not His.

In times when Sallie felt better, she would encourage me to return to work. But it was always difficult to pull myself away. We'd spent far too many years apart because of the demands of my work and my activism. I'd try to tell her how much I depended on her to ground me, even when we were apart. She was so wise, always the smartest girl in class, always the prettiest too.

Since leaving the White House, I'd been invited to serve on the boards of many top corporations and organizations. (The most shocking one had to be the North Carolina Railroad, the same railroad my great-grandfather had been forced to build as a slave, a century earlier.) I was torn about accepting these positions because of Sallie's continuing health struggle, but most of them paid well

and the meetings weren't all that frequent. I could take on less client work that way, which meant, overall, I had more time to be with
Sallie.

I was attending a board meeting for AutoNation at its corporate headquarters in Fort Lauderdale, when Sallie took a turn for
the worse in the late 1990s. When I told the company's founder,
Wayne Huizenga, that I had to leave the board meeting because
Sallie's cancer had resurfaced, he asked what I planned to do. I said
that I hoped to catch the first flight home, pick her up, and then
book another flight to New York, where I'd made her an appointment at Memorial Sloan Kettering Cancer Center.

"Oh, hell no, Bob," said Wayne.

He turned to his executive assistant and said, "Call our corporate pilots and tell them to prepare the jet. Get a driver to take Bob
to our airport hangar. They will fly him to North Carolina to get
Sallie, then fly them to New York City, and stay with them until
Bob doesn't need them anymore."

Sallie and I were blessed to have friends like Wayne, who passed
away as I was completing this book. Sallie battled her cancer until
she could fight no more. She died on February 22, 2004, at the age
of sixty-seven. We'd been married forty-seven years, and losing her
threw me into an unrelenting darkness. Depression and grief made
it difficult for me to even leave the house. I couldn't focus on work,
nor could I sleep more than a few hours at a time.

Grief is something else altogether, I'll tell you. It weighs so
heavy on your soul. Sallie was my grade school girlfriend, my teen-
age love, my soul mate, my business partner, my traveling compan-
ion, and the foundation of everything I did. I had loved her for so
long, I didn't know how to live without her. Our friends and family members supported me and visited and consoled me, but there
is no consoling someone in that kind of pain. Time really is the
only relief. The more time that passes, the duller the pain, though
it never goes away.

For all of the powerful and celebrated men I've worked with in my lifetime, I often think about the fact that my greatest influences have been the humble and strong women who have inspired, motivated, and loved me. I think about my grandmother, Miss Nellie Brown, who took me in when my birth mother lost her way; who raised me and my brother, Bill, with a fortifying love, a guiding wisdom, and a belief that "life is about giving and serving." I think about my Sallie, the pretty little girl in the first pew at church, the smartest girl seated at the front of the classroom, the beautiful bride who always encouraged me to be the best man I could be, the partner in life who never let me get bigheaded and full of myself, even as she guarded my back and steered me straight. I still miss her every day and I still hear her voice, especially when I have to make a tough decision.

Now, Robert . . .

Conclusion

SMUGGLING AND OTHER GOOD DEEDS

A S I WRITE THIS IN THE SPRING OF 2018, I AM EIGHTY-THREE years old. My wife, Sallie, has been gone fourteen years. Our country has seen a black man serve two terms as president of the United States, and I have attended far too many funerals of my friends from the civil rights days, my White House years, and my South African connections.

I've just returned from the funeral for Winnie Mandela, who died April 2, 2018, at the age of eighty-one. She was an amazing woman, who rose from utter poverty to become a true freedom fighter and champion of her people, though often misunderstood.

I know the feeling, yet I am not bitter, nor am I discouraged. I am still energized and engaged, still working with clients, and still doing what I can to support equal opportunity and social justice. I am content and ever determined to remain behind the scenes as the bridge builder and problem solver. I've shared my experiences with you because I hope you will do whatever you can to serve the greater good that most inspires you to action.

Do it for the right reasons, and don't let anyone discourage you. Or as my grandmother, my beloved Miss Nellie, would say, "Let go and let God . . . Don't let nobody turn you 'round."

I have known many remarkable men and women over the years. I still shake my head in wonder at how I came to be in the company of so many truly charismatic, inspiring, faith-filled, dedicated, and accomplished people. Most of them came from humble origins. A great many of them came from desperate circumstances. Some went through hell and back, yet they persevered and rose to achieve incredible things.

My own life has had its share of mountains and valleys too. I've found that my best strategy is not to dwell too much on either the victories or the defeats, but instead to push on, to keep serving those people and causes that matter to me, instead of focusing on myself. I've written of the recurring pattern in my life in which I find myself in the middle of two opposing forces, trying to bring them together for good. This, I believe, is a result of another underlying theme in my life: my inner battle with anger, rooted in the racism and injustice I've seen and endured. This is a battle that most black men and women carry within them.

Nelson Mandela and the Reverend Martin Luther King Jr. were masters of using their faith to control and channel their anger into energy to drive themselves to do good. Dr. King, who often talked and wrote of the rage within himself, called his method of controlling it "creative nonviolence." He used the negative emotions for positive means. This has been my way too, and the way of most men and women of achievement. We surrender our anger to God, trusting in faith that He will use it for good.

Prayer is still important to me. God has been good. I've had my trials and stayed in faith even in times when anger and despair have brought me to my knees. I've encountered true evil, stood face-to-face with it, more times than I care to remember. Yet I am blessed for all of the good in my life, the miracles I've witnessed, the generous and kind women and men I have known and continue to meet.

My encouragement to you is to be open to every opportunity to share your gifts and talents, and to leave this world a better place. By now, you know that one of Mama's favorite mantras was "You can't go wrong doing right." I've tried to follow her guidance, but before I leave you, I should confess that for a time in South Africa, I did right by doing something wrong—at least according to President Botha and his henchmen.

I like to think this was an act of creative nonviolence in the face of evil. You see, beginning in the late 1980s, I became a smuggler, importing banned materials into South Africa and distributing them covertly to poor black residents in the vast, segregated townships.

At first, my operation fell within the laws of apartheid, because I only brought in regular shipments of clothing, food, and school supplies for the needy residents. Over time, however, I began including prohibited materials with the other goods.

I was inspired to do this after a visit one day to the Soweto township library, run by Patience Maisela. She worked in a brick building of no more than 400 square feet in the impoverished township. There were five shelves and usually not enough books to fill them. This was the only library serving the township's population of more than 700,000 people.

The Soweto library triggered memories of the scanty shelves in the "Negro library" of my youth in High Point. There was a bigger, fully stocked public library across town, but it was whites-only. The library for blacks had far fewer books, but I still had more books to choose from than hundreds of thousands of poor children in Soweto.

As an avid reader since childhood, it pained me to see so many young people deprived of this most basic opportunity to learn. I first asked Patience if there was anything I could provide that might help her run the library. She politely said she could use a typewriter, because she had to go to the other side of Johannesburg to type library cards and letters. It took her an entire day to do that, since she had to ride a series of buses there and back while passing through police checkpoints, which was always dangerous.

"Before the sun sets tomorrow, you will have a typewriter," I promised.

I made certain that a typewriter was sent to her. Then I asked what more I could do to help. Patience said she had tried to bring in books for her library, but the white South African government made it difficult, if not impossible. When American church groups sent books, the authorities would send them back, citing a law that said it was illegal. I thought about how in my country it had once been illegal to teach black slaves to read. Many learned to read anyway. My ancestors were among them.

Even in my school days, we received hand-me-down schoolbooks from the white kids' schools. They came to us with pages torn out, covers ripped off, and someone else's notes scrawled in the margins. In college, I remember feeling a sense of liberation when I first put my hands on a new book with a shiny cover and crisp white pages. I wanted to give South African children that same feeling.

And so, my smuggling career began.

My illegal acts of defiance began with a few books stashed in my personal luggage. I cheerfully lied to the customs inspectors about the contents of my bags. "I'm trying to catch up with my reading on the long plane trip." But the more I thought about the book ban, the angrier I got and the larger my shipments became. Within months, I began sending books in shipping containers. I told South African Airways the containers were filled with clothes and toys for the children in the squatter camps. It was a small lie. There were always clothes, shoes, and a few toys in every box, just like I said. They didn't need to know that those supplies also came along with hundreds of books.

I'd rent a truck and have the containers delivered to Kennedy Airport in New York City. Smaller trucks driven by my co-conspirators met my plane upon arrival in South Africa. Successful businessman and philanthropist Linda Twala, known as the "father of Alexandra Township," was one of my main accomplices. He always brought a crew of workers to help distribute the items I'd shipped over.

We would drive to distribution points within Soweto and other

black townships, and children would run behind the trucks, calling to their parents and friends to alert them: "Papa Brown is here!
Papa Brown!" Long lines were formed by the time we parked and
began unloading and organizing everything for distribution. It was
like handing out hope to a people desperate for something positive
in their lives.

I was often overcome with emotion, as were Linda Twala and
the others who volunteered to help us. We were so wrapped up in
the moment in those early days that I'd forget about the potential
dangers. Linda and other black South Africans warned me that
the apartheid government might send their thugs to beat me, jail
me, or worse if they caught me distributing books. I tried to be
discreet, but such large crowds gathered for the book distributions
that it was difficult to hide what we were doing.

We'd been getting away with it for a year or so before there was
a serious confrontation. I'd set up a distribution point for shoes,
clothing, food items, and books in Alexandra township, near a
health clinic Linda had built. I'd had two large shipping containers trucked in. We were surrounded by stacks of canned goods,
bottled water, medical supplies, and books. A huge crowd was
gathered, and there were several lines extending for thirty or forty
yards each.

The mood was festive. There was singing and laughter. People
helped each other carry goods back to their homes. And then we
heard the roar of two military trucks driving through the crowd.
There was nowhere for us to hide as the government security soldiers piled out with their rifles and pistols pointed at us and the
people we had drawn.

A tall white officer carrying a leather riding crop walked up and
got in my face. "Why are all these people here with you?" he demanded. We weren't quite eyeball-to-eyeball, but we were close.

There were stacks of books all around me. Lying was not an
option, and besides, righteous anger was making my blood boil.

"Don't worry about the books," I said. "I'm in charge here."

"Are you selling something?" he barked.

"No, I'm giving away clothes, shoes, food, and books," I said.

"Books! Where did these books come from?"

"I brought them from America," I said.

"We don't allow any books here," he shouted angrily in my face. He looked as though he wanted to grab my throat and choke me to death right there.

"Yes sir, I've heard that, but I brought them anyway."

The officer appeared to be nearing a meltdown, so I showed him my passport as a distraction. He jerked it out of my hand.

"Here are my papers," I said. "I'd suggest you call the foreign minister's office or the president's office and check my credentials. I'm not someone you should be playing with. If you mess with what I'm doing here, there will be more trouble than you want to deal with."

For a moment, it seemed like he actually might try to hit me with his little whip. I was prepared to shove it down his throat. My adrenaline was pumping, and I had one hand wrapped around my push-button switchblade knife in my jacket pocket. If he made a move to strike me or ordered his men to shoot into the crowd, I was prepared to stab him in the heart.

Instead, he walked back to his truck with my passport in hand. He got inside and we could hear him talking loudly over his radio in Afrikaans. There was a back-and-forth conversation for ten or fifteen minutes as he read my passport information to the other person, likely a superior.

At the end, I heard him shout, *"Jah! Jah! Jah!"* Then he got out of the truck cab, walked back to me, and handed back my passport.

"Sir! Here's your passport. It's okay to hand out clothes, shoes and socks, but sir, do not bring books back into this country! Do not do that!"

I gave him a defiant stare, but kept my tone polite and deferential because I just wanted him to leave without hurting any of those gathered.

"Thank you. I appreciate that," I said.

The soldiers filed back into their trucks and drove away. Nobody in the crowd said a word. They had been frightened for their lives, and hadn't dared to breathe.

I fully expected to be dogged by the security troops after that, but they never bothered me again, even when huge crowds showed up. Over time, many supporters—both corporate and private—stepped in, and our humble book program grew into a much bigger operation. I believe we've distributed more than nine million books to this day.

The experience taught me a lesson that I suppose I've been learning all my life: When you decide to do something that benefits others in need, you'll almost certainly face resistance. But if you keep at it, your good work will attract supporters who believe in what you are doing.

As the white leaders of South Africa eventually learned, revolution is bred in the ghettos when education and equal opportunities are denied. It is no longer possible to enslave the minds and bodies of a people and escape condemnation from the rest of the world.

I HOPE READING this book, about a child rising from poverty to accomplish some good in this world, will inspire others from difficult circumstances to put their faith in God and then do all they can to elevate their lives.

Where I am weak, God is strong. I know that is true for me, and I believe it is true for us all. Please, know that as long as you have faith, as long as you put your hand in God's hands, He will take you as far as you dare to dream, maybe even beyond. I was lucky to have men and women in my life who built me up, who showed me that I was worthy of love and capable of great things. Words have the power to inspire and motivate, yet they can also tear you apart if you let them. Choose carefully those words that you decide to act upon; you have the power to do that, and it is an important power.

I will leave you with some of the homespun advice that carried me through good times and bad, the lessons Miss Nellie Brown passed on across the kitchen table, in the garden, from her chair on the front porch, and on the walks to and from church.

If you take them into your heart and live by them, I'm certain they will help you just as they've helped me.

1. *You never know which way the Lord is coming at you.*
2. *You are not a problem. You are a prize. The Lord doesn't make mistakes.*
3. *The best way to influence others is to be helpful.*
4. *You can't go wrong doing right.*
5. *Wherever you go, stay humble and let God go first.*
6. *Give whatever you've got, because you can't out-give God.*
7. *Never forget that you were put on this Earth to do something bigger than you.*
8. *You can find good anywhere and do good everywhere.*
9. *Life is about giving and serving.*
10. *I dare you to trust God!*
11. *When bad things happen, let it go and let God handle it. Don't let nobody turn you around!*

Acknowledgments

To the many associates, friends, and extended family with whom I have shared in the various stages of my life and in the creation of this book, I offer a heart full of gratitude and appreciation for the experiences we have shared and the contributions you have made to my story and to my life.

You all have been a major part of my journey. For that, I am eternally grateful. God bless each one of you.

This book project was undertaken over the course of more than a decade, and I would especially like to thank my literary agent, Jan Miller Rich of Dupree Miller & Associates, for her loyalty over all those years.

I offer thanks also to my writing collaborator and friend Wes Smith, who assisted me from the very beginning, spending hundreds of hours doing research and interviews, and helping me through countless drafts and revisions.

My thanks also to my editors at Convergent: Derek Reed and David Kopp.

Others who've been of tremendous help in my career, my life, and with this book include:

Brenda Williams	*Stedman Graham*
Johnnie Kirkland	*Oprah Winfrey*
James McNeil	*Bob Wright*
Arthur Marshall	*Armstrong Williams*
Lenette Burris	*Tony Welters*

Mike Jackson

Mary Douglas

Barbara Fisher

Sammie Chess

James Patterson

Dr. Burdell Knight

Osyris Uqoezwa

Terry Giroux

Carole Hoover

Evan Walker

Dave Stewart

Ambassador Bonnie Hunter

Rev. Otis Moss

Harold Burson

Dr. Nido Qubein

Verdie Kendall

Bishop George Battle

Jean Daniels

Roy Carr

Valeria Simpson

George Faison

Dr. Otis and Mrs. Barbara Tillman

Mahalia Hines

Harris DeLoach

Mac Everett

Rev. Andrew Young

Rev. Joseph Lowery

Dr. Jimmy Jenkins

David Miller

Dr. Ronald Carter

Lydia Stuckey

Dwain Skeen

Dr. Johnetta Cole

Dr. Maxine Mimms

Dr. Lenny Peters

Linda Twala

Alex Rizos

Thomas Stith

Larry Yon

Paul Fulton

Elynor Williams

Ned Covington

Gary Grom

John Bryan

Mary Griffin

Roy Ackerman

Lois Hobson

Bryan Pember

Governor Pat McCrory

Dean Ronald Phillips

Earl and Kitty Congdon

Frank Harrison

Louis and Aldona DeJoy

Larry Shaw

Evelyn Shaw

William H. Brown

Dr. Kenneth Kaunda

Earl G. Graves Sr.

Mayor Johnny Ford

Gordon Collins

Christine Farris

Sam Wylie

Don Rumsfeld

John Cardone

Doug Holladay

Charles Coker

Mark Morial

Bruce Rabb

Terry Giles

Dr. Tom Haggai

Justice Clarence Thomas

Willie Davis

Rev. Jessie Jackson

Rev. Barbara Skinner

King Goodwill Zewelithini

Rev. Michael Ola

*His Royal Highness
    Adewale Shotobi*

Betty Dikko

Arnold Mentz

Jimmy Pattison

Monica Mngadi

Carole Weatherford

Mary Douglas

David Stein

George Shultz

Julius Erving

Lee Elder

Rose Elder

Mamie Jacobs

John Jacobs

Hugh Price

Gayle King

Ron Walker

Lloyd Price

President George H. W. Bush

President George W. Bush

General Colin Powell

Isyaku Ibrahim

William H. Brown

Quincy Jones

Dick Cheney

Senator Robert Dole

Senator Elizabeth Dole

David and Julie Eisenhower

Ed and Tricia Cox

Barry Saunders

President Shehu Shagari

President Barack Obama

Vic and Don Flow

Earl and Kitty Congdon

David Congdon

Jim Morgan

Harold Martin

Garth Reeves

Dr. Alvin Schexnider

John Cardone

*North Carolina Supreme
    Court Justices Henry
    Frye and Shirley Frye*

LeRoy Sellers

Dr. William McCray

Lawrence Graves

Dr. Jimmy Jenkins

Nicholas Perkins

Governor Jim Martin

Chris Tucker

Al Campbell

James Jett

*Hon. Constance Berry
    Newman*

David Steward

Melvyn N. Klein

Dr. L'Tanya Joy Bailey

Lee Thomas Broadie

As you can imagine with a project that went on for so many years, more than a few of those close to me have passed on. I would like to acknowledge them as important figures of my life as well. They include:

Bishop Arthur Marshall

Wayne Huizenga

Nelson and Winnie Mandela

Alex Haley

Loretta Marshall

Sammy Davis Jr.

Dr. Maya Angelou

Ernest Nathan "Dutch"
*   Morial*

John Mack

Dr. Eddie Smith

Joseph W. Daniels Sr.

George and Shirley Rhodes

Nick Ashford

Sam Sparks

Barbara Hildreth

Gracie Reese

Marcus Brown

President Richard M. Nixon

Robert Woods

George Hammond

S. S. Whitted

Rosetta Baldwin

Rev. Warren Steele

Senator O. Arthur Kirkman

Dr. Martin Luther King Jr.

Rev. Odie Hoover

Samuel Burford

Ethel Hughes

Dr. Umaru Dikko

Jack and Marsha Slane

Thurmond Woodard

Mick Quinn

Ethel Wilson

Louis Haizlip

Clarence Townes

Ray Boone

Fred Brown

A. G. Gaston

Tom A. Finch

Joseph M. Hunt Jr.

O. H. Leak

Herman Russell

Felton Capel

Dr. Otis Wells

John Johnson

Jessie Hill

James Brown

Willie Mason

Arthur Fletcher

Della Ingram
Dr. Perry Little
Stanley Scott
Rev. W. E. Banks
Rev. Ralph Abernathy
Dorothy I. Height
Fannie Lou Hamer
Johnnie Booker Sr.
Dick Gregory
Rev. Billy Kyles
Rev. B. Elton Cox
Golden Frinks
Billie Armfield
Mr. and Mrs. William
    McGuinn
General Frank Peterson
General Chappie James
Ed Moseley

Peter Peterson
Max and Patience Maisela
Emperor Haile Selassie
Mr. and Mrs. Truett Cathey
John Wheeler
Mose Kiser Sr.
Buford Bailey
Walter Washington
John Wilkes
Herb Cline
Roy Carr
George Paul
Andrew Hatcher
James Farmer
Senator Ed Brooke
Jackie Robinson
Admiral John McCain
Mayor Andrew Hatcher